Battlegrou...

GOMMECOURT

Battleground Europe

GOMMECOURT

Nigel Cave

Series editor
Nigel Cave

LEO COOPER

First published in 1998 by
LEO COOPER
an imprint of
Pen Sword Books Limited
47 Church Street, Barnsley, South Yorkshire S70 2AS

ISBN 0 85052 561 6

A CIP catalogue of this book is available
from the British Library

Printed by Redwood Books Limited
Trowbridge, Wiltshire

*For up-to-date information on other titles produced under the Leo Cooper imprint,
please telephone or write to:*

Pen & Sword Books Ltd, FREEPOST, 47 Church Street
Barnsley, South Yorkshire S70 2AS
Telephone 01226 734555

CONTENTS

~ Dedication ~

*This book is dedicated to
the memory of Harry
Roberts MM, who served in
a Field Ambulance in the
46th (North Midland)
Division for the bulk of the
war. I had the privilege of
enjoying his friendship in
his last years, and will
forever remember
discussing the war - and
other things - over his
'world famous Stilton and
peaches and cream teas'.
He was a wonderful,
friendly gentleman. May he
rest in peace.*

ACKNOWLEDGEMENTS

This book is largely based on the material provided by the historians of regiments and divisions; and by the Official Historian. These histories can be of variable quality, but there was a particularly rich seam to mine in the array of histories produced by the battalions of the two Territorial divisions with which I was chiefly concerned at Gommecourt.

For other material I am indebted to Ralph Whitehead of New York State, USA for German translations and illustrations; to Norbert Krüger of Essen in Germany for the loan of much valuable material; to Jim Walton for information and illustrations on the Tamworth Territorials, part of 6/North Staffords; to Colonel Pat Love and the Worcesters RHQ for material relating to the Rev Tanner, MC*; to the RHQ of the RAMC at Millbank for the use of the painting of Captain Green's VC action as a cover for this book; to Robert and Margaret Tedd for material relating to Margaret's father, Harry Roberts MM; and to Bill Mitchinson for permission to use some of his maps produced for his book *Gentlemen and Officers.*

Particular thanks are due to Richard Brucciani, who has once more given of his time and his plane to fly me over the battlefields, thereby enabling me to make the most of the possibilities of aerial photography.

Various people have accompanied me on shorter or longer visits to this particular battlefield; my sister, Jackie; my father, Colonel Terry Cave, along with Colonel Dick Burge and Wing Commander Martin Sparkes; and during a frantic weekend of commemoration ceremonies at Beaumont Hamel and Vimy in November 1997, Colonel Phillip Robinson and his wife Mary. To them all many thanks for patience, interest and companionship.

On my visits to the Somme I have traditionally stayed with Mike and Julie Renshaw at their famously comfortable Bed and Breakfast accommodation, Les Galets, in Auchonvillers; and I have also descended upon Avril Williams and her family in their similar establishment in the same village, and enjoyed some excellent baguette lunches.

I have continued to enjoy working with Roni Wilkinson at Pen and Sword, who continues to put so much effort into making this series of books work; it is good to see the tradition continued by his son, Paul.

As ever I am grateful for the first class service offered by the staff of the Commonwealth War Graves Commission, who have patiently answered questions and supplied me with registers on their admirable loan system. I would in particular like to pay tribute in this book to Beverley Webb, who retired from the CWGC in the autumn of 1997.

I am also grateful to the farmers of the Gommecourt area who seem now to be able to take in their stride the sight of British registered vehicles in places where no vehicle in its right mind should be. Invariably they have managed to wave cheerily - probably anything to avoid contact with the mad British!

Finally grateful thanks to many of the 'regulars' that I meet in France and Belgium who provide welcoming faces or, in the case of Janet Fairgrieve at Delville Wood, the joys of a glorious cup of coffee. All of them make trips over there a real pleasure.

ADVICE TO TOURERS

Access to the battlefield from Calais is usually via the A26, and then on to the A1 (Paris) autoroutes. Your exit can be either near Monchy, to the south east of Arras or at Bapaume. The latter will allow you a drive over the northern part of the Somme Battlefield. Follow the D929 towards Albert and then turn right in Pozieres, following the signs for Thiepval and the Newfoundland Park. You might wish to make an early stop at both the hugely impressive Thiepval Memorial and, later on, the Park. The Newfoundland Park will give you at least an impression of the look of a Somme battlefield, albeit now a rural idyll surrounded by trees. From here continue towards Puisieux and in this village take the turning to either Hebuterne or Gommecourt.

For touring purposes you will find the French IGN Green series most useful - in this case 4 Laon Arras. For the detailed work around Gommecourt it would be most helpful to be equipped with the IGN Blue Series (1:25000) 2407 Bapaume Ouest. These maps are usually available in Libraire; there are a couple of these in the square in front of the Basilica in Albert. There are also 1:250000 maps overprinted with the locations of Commonwealth War Grave Cemeteries which is available from the CWGC in Maidenhead, details of telephone and address appear later in this section. The maps cost £3 at the time of writing. The interested might want to get the relevant trench maps; the best way of doing this is to become a member of the Western Front Association, which runs a trench map service (and from whom, incidentally, you may also purchase the Blue IGN maps). The ones that you require are the 1:10000 Fonquevillers 57D NE Sheets 1 & 2 dated 27.12.16 and Hebuterne 57D NE Sheets 3 & 4 dated 26.8.16 There is also available a 1:5000 map, extremely detailed of the German lines, Misc 018 probably dated June 1916. Information about membership of the WFA may be obtained from: The Membership Secretary, 17, Aldrin Way, Cannon Park, Coventry CV4 7DP. Please enclose a large SAE.

Gommecourt is a very open area, and it is easy to get very hot (or very cold!) so it is important that if you are going to go on a long walk to wear suitable clothing (most notably some sort of hat) and to carry plenty of water. There are plenty of places to sit down and have a picnic (that is, if it is dry). The bigger cemeteries usually have some sort of shelter, but if the weather is that bad you would be best to head for a café. It is easy to buy the necessaries for a picnic, but do not forget the plastic mug and the corkscrew! I would recommend that you wear walking boots - wellingtons are not usually good for medium distances, and the ground is rarely that bad.

You will need a camera and I would suggest that it should have some sort of telephoto facility. You should take a notebook to record details of photographs taken, as one field looks very much like another. If you are going to photograph gravestones, then a tripod would be useful, and if you are looking for a particular name on the Thiepval Memorial this suggestion and that relating to a telephoto lens is even more relevant - the top of a column of names at Thiepval can be a long way. Binoculars, in particular on this battlefield, will be very useful, as will a compass.

The walks around Gommecourt are restricted by the fact that a lot of the tracks go so far and then stop, sometimes tantalisingly close to another track that would produce a nice round route. The rules are simple, and are as for the UK. Farmers depend for their livelihood on their fields, and if there is no obvious track, then do not go trampling

Felix-Faure Street in Albert.

over the crops. Obviously there are times of the year when no damage would be done, but please do not ignore the rights of others. The woods in the area are private and you should keep out of them unless you have permission. They can also be extremely hazardous, especially when shooting gets under way in the late summer and the autumn. A lot of the hunters behave in what we would find a cavalier fashion as regards safety and a number of people are injured or even killed every year through shooting accidents. The best advice is keep well clear of woods. At certain times, especially after harvest, even the fields can be risky, especially on a Sunday when the world and his wife seem to be out shooting with their dogs. Please also be aware that the tracks are there for a purpose, and farmers can understandably get extremely irritated by thoughtless parking; obviously it does not matter if you are close to the vehicle, but do not leave a car blocking a track and then disappear on a long walk.

There are still a lot of munitions unearthed every year. They still kill - in fact I know of two fatalities in 1997. Leave them alone; the French attitude may seem fairly relaxed, with piles of shells by the road, but this should not mean that you do not treat them with just as much respect as if you dug up a grenade in your garden. Safe souvenirs can be purchased at Delville Wood and the museum in Albert should you so wish.

Several places of interest should be combined with a visit to the battlefield. Before you go I would recommend both the Imperial War Museum and the National Army Museum in London. Both of them

Shells awaiting collection by the bomb disposal squad.

The Basilica in Albert with the river Ancre on the left.
TAYLOR LIBRARY

provide an excellent introduction to any tour that you might make. The Imperial War Museum also has a massive photographic library, a sound archive and a library (as does the NAM). An appointment is required (but easily obtained) from the IWM for these facilities, and a Readers' Ticket for the NAM library. There are several good museums on the Somme area. One particularly fine one is adjacent to the National Cemetery at Notre Dame de Lorette, near Vimy Ridge; there are excellent tableaux (with sound effects and commentary in English), wonderful uniform displays, photographs and the like. Nearer to Gommecourt is the war museum housed in the old air raid shelters in Albert - entrance is by the side of the famous basilica. This comparatively new venture is improving all the time and is well worth an hour of your time. There is also the very fine museum at Peronne, the Historial; this can take a long time to study in depth, but is well worth the drive to this town well below the British part of the Somme battlefield. On the Somme battlefield itself I would strongly recommend a visit to the South African Memorial at Delville Wood. Besides an impressive memorial and museum, there is a small coffee shop run by Mrs Janet Fairgrieve which sells soft drinks, tea and coffee and confectionery; it also has a good range of books for sale about the war as well as souvenirs. Outside there is plentiful seating space for picnics and there are also comfortable and clean toilets.

If you are tracing a relative, or have any interest in people buried during the Great War, then the Commonwealth War Graves Commission can supply you with details. It is important that you give them as much information as possible - preferably full name, regiment, battalion, date and location of death (ie France and Flanders, Italy or whatever). A charge may be levied, according to circumstances. The address for the CWGC is 2, Marlow Road, Maidenhead, Berks Tel 01628 634221. There is also an office at Beaurains, on the southern outskirts of Arras, and they hold the same records. The CWGC does an enormously impressive job, and it would be appreciated if you took the time to fill in the Visitors' Book which is found in all the cemeteries except the smallest; in these times of financial stringency the number of recorded visitors adds to the CWGC cause when the time comes to plead for funding.

For your vehicle you should have the registration document and a copy of your insurance - a Green Card is not usually required now for France, but check with your insurers. A First Aid kit, spare light bulbs and a warning triangle are all compulsory. The French police are quite keen on spot checks, so do not forget your driving licence either. It is probably worthwhile pointing out that French drink driving laws are now stricter than those in the UK (though there are rumours that the UK ones will also be changed to a lower limit).

For yourself and any passengers I would strongly recommend full personal medical and health insurance, though the form E 1 11, available from main post offices, does give reciprocal cover. Ensure that you take the standard medications with you, and given the amount of rusty iron lying around, an up to date tetanus jab would be sensible. In the summer sun cream is a must, and the winds can whip up, so the appropriate salve for your lips would be useful.

Theft from cars is not unusual, and so please follow the standard sensible precautions.

Gommecourt is right at the northernmost part of the 1916 Somme battlefield; it is a small village of maybe 100 inhabitants; not surprisingly, it has no cafes or other facilities - it is very much a farming community. Fonquevillers to the north west is an altogether bigger place, although only abut 400 people live there. However, it boasts the only hotel in the immediate vicinity and has a small café where you can get something to eat, as well as a garage and petrol station. Garages are indeed quite rare in this part of the world, so I suppose that I should thank my lucky stars that the one time that I have broken down in France happened to be just outside the village. The fact that there is an adjacent café was an added bonus, as it took several hours to repair and I also happened to have a bus load of fourteen year old pupils with me, who were, on reflection, enormously patient; certainly the people in Fonquevillers could not have been more helpful. It also served to remind how useful it is to carry spare parts - in this case a drive belt for a Mercedes minibus! Hebuterne is also a large village by Somme standards, and boasts a café as well, so the visitor to this part of the battlefields is unusually well catered for, at least on the refreshment side. Should you wish to do some shopping for essentials for the picnic, Bucquoy has a small supermarket at its northern end (the place seems to go on for ever) and a petrol station with some of the cheapest prices around. Shopping hours can be different to the UK (for instance get there before lunchtime on a Saturday), so be warned. There are, of course, extensive supermarkets in Albert.

Accommodation can be had easily in Arras, which is almost as close as Albert, the traditional base for a Somme tour. There are also a large number of bed and breakfasts in the area, run by British couples as well as by French people. The following is just a sample - a fuller list is available from the Comité Regional du Tourisme de Picardie, 3 Rue Vincent Auriol, 80000 Amiens. Tel 00 33 322 91 10 15

HOTELS:
The Royal Picardie, Route d'Amiens, 80300 Albert
Tel 33 322 75 37 00
Hotel de la Basilique, 3-5 Rue Gambetta, 80300
Tel 322 75 04 71
Relais Fleuri, 56 Avenue Faidherbe, 80300 Albert
Tel 322 75 08 11
Grande Hotel de la Paix, 43 Rue Victor Hugo, 80300 Albert
Tel 322 75 01 64.

I have stayed in this latter hotel on many occasions and have found it tremendously friendly with an excellent restaurant. 'Uncle Fred', the proprietor, and his wife, who did so much to make one feel at home, have recently retired, but the hotel has remained in the family and I am assured that the tradition continues.

B&B style accommodation: these can be seasonal and closed over some of the winter months (usually after the 11th November commemorations) so please check first before you set off if you are planning a winter tour.

Auchonvillers:

Les Galets, Route de Beaumont, 80560 Auchonvillers
Tel/Fax 322 76 28 79.

This house, run by Julie and Mike Renshaw, is just behind the old British front line before Beaumont Hamel. It is ideal for anyone wanting interesting walks along parts of the 1916 front - whether over Redan Ridge or to the Newfoundland Park. The rooms are all en suite, the breakfast is substantial, evening meals are available on a number of days during the week and there are comfortable sitting areas and lovely grounds.

Avril Williams, 10, Rue de Lattre, 80560 Auchonvillers.
This is a large former farmhouse in the village, with a most interesting cellar and a proprietress who bubbles over with enthusiasm. The rooms are all en suite, and a substantial breakfast is served. Evening meals (also substantial) are available. There is now a bar, and this is a good place to get a baguette and beer at lunchtime.

Rather further afield, but with a resident battlefield expert, is *Sommecourt, 39 Grande Rue, 80300 Courcelette Tel/Fax 322 74 01 35.* The house is ideally placed for those who might also wish to explore the later stages of the Somme in Courcelette itself or Pozieres.

There is very comfortable accommodation in Mailly Maillet in one of the first houses on the right as one enters this very large village on the D919 heading towards Amiens. This also has a cellar with a most interesting history, and the son of the proprietress has an encyclopaedic knowledge of the history of the place. Gite accommodation and B&B, also French run, is available quite reasonably in Grandcourt, on the banks of the Ancre.

I can most strongly recommend the Auberge in Authuille if you are after a good quality French meal not too far from the Gommecourt battlefield site.

This great list is not meant to deter or make it sound as though you are going on a mission to the Amazon; but the advice is culled from many years of battlefield touring and is designed to make your time trouble free and enjoyable.

HOW TO USE THIS BOOK

For those who have never visited the Battlefields I would recommend that you sit down with this book (and one or two others that I have recommended in the Further Reading section) to get a feel for the events and for the ground. This book is primarily concerned with a battle that lasted on one flank all of a few minutes and on the other for the hours of daylight but a lot was happening in that time. The best way to tour this particular battlefield is by bicycle, largely because of the layout of the tracks and their quality. Some tracks start off most encouragingly, but can then peter out to nothing - and with no obvious way of getting back out again except by a mildly hair-raising exercise in reversing. The next best method is by a combination of car and walking. The soldier saw the ground on foot, so naturally this is the best way to appreciate their view of the battlefield. On the other hand, it needs to be remembered that they saw it from several feet down in the ground, and this significantly qualifies the view that they saw.

At the back of the book there is a section on car and walking tours. You would be advised to follow the car route around so that you can get your bearings before engaging on the more detailed tours. In this book the references to cemeteries and memorials are incorporated within the tours, but the index can be used if you get to one of these outside of a tour.

The book is a guide to the Gommecourt battlefield - it is not even fully inclusive of all the material available on that. It does not set out to be a critical examination of this part of the Somme, nor even of this battle; other books are readily available for what is probably the most written about battle in British military history, with all the controversies that follow on from this wealth of printed matter. What I would urge you to do, as you walk these fields, is consider the problem not only from the view of those men in the trenches who did the fighting, but also the considerable difficulties facing their staffs and commanders. The secondary aim of the book is to be thought provoking and to invite re-examination of whatever prejudices about the Great War that we might have.

GOMMECOURT MAPS

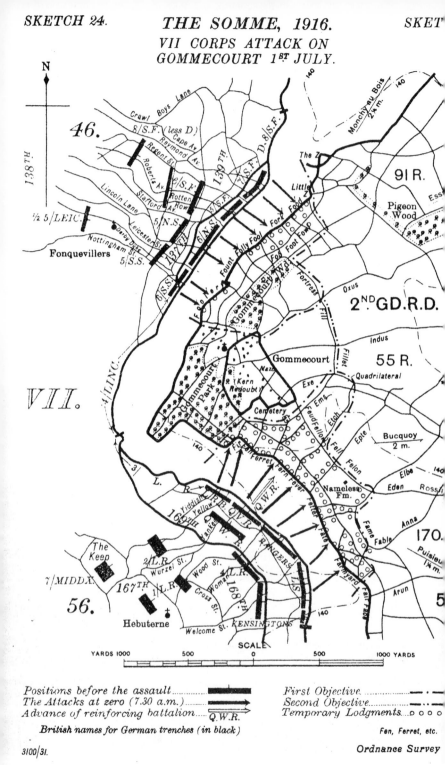

Map 1. VII Corps attack on Gommecourt.

INTRODUCTION

Gommecourt is a typically sleepy Somme village, protected to its west and north by woodland. In the summer of 1916 it was under German occupation, occupying a quite pronounced salient in the line with reputedly the westernmost point of German occupation in France being marked by the 'Kaiser's Oak' at the extremity of Gommecourt Park.

On 1 July the village was to be the objective of two of the Territorial divisions serving in the British Expeditionary Force - the 56th and the 46th, the former consisting of London regiments and the latter those from the North Midlands. The attack was to be a diversion from the main thrust of the Anglo-French onslaught, which was to stretch from the hamlet of Serre in the north to Montauban in the south. The main battle came under the command of General Sir Henry Rawlinson's Fourth Army; the attack on Gommecourt under General Sir Edmund Allenby's Third Army.

The aim of this diversion was, at the least, to divert German men and equipment from the 'Big Push' and to keep them uncertain of the extent of the allied attack. The action at Serre, where the aim of the British was to act as a hinge for the general breakthrough further south, was particularly fraught, and thus the diversion was seen as essential if the Germans were not to concentrate resources on this seemingly insignificant part of France. A minor bonus, if success was achieved, would be the removal of a not particularly troublesome salient into the

Gommecourt, looking East. In the foreground is Gommecourt Park, to its left rear Gommecourt Wood and in the middle distance Pigeon Wood.

WELL MET!

GREAT BRITAIN JOINS HER ALLIES IN THE FIELD.

As far as the French were concerned, it was about time in July 1916 that the British put some of the pressure on the Germans.

British lines. Certainly there was absolutely no intention of following up any success, as there were no troops available.

If a diversionary attack had to be launched, Gommecourt was not a particularly suitable spot - it was a well-established German stronghold, the two divisions were recent arrivals to the place (they took over the line in mid May 1916), and if captured positions had to be evacuated, the line of withdrawal was highly vulnerable to German fire. Allenby and VII Corps commander (Snow) both suggested that Arras would be a better place to attract German reserves and artillery - a view with which the Official History concurs, although even this document, generally critical of the Gommecourt attack, is forced to conclude that such an action, 'would not have prevented the enemy from using the guns which he had in the vicinity of Gommecourt against the northern flank of VIII Corps (attacking at Serre).'

The Germans had fortified Gommecourt extensively, partly because of its naturally strong defensive position and partly because of attempts by the French earlier in the war to oust them. Dugouts were particularly deep (many forty feet and more, with electricity and kitchens), interconnected and with tunnels to the rear; there was defence in depth, with a couple of switch lines; a very strong redoubt (the Maze to the British, Kern Redoubt to the Germans); and reinforced communication trenches that meant that a well-disciplined garrison could contain a breakthrough in any part of the sector.

The British intended to launch their attack at the base of the Gommecourt salient and then join up in the rear, using the German Ist Switch Line as their meeting and consolidation position. This meant that the village proper (and the troublesome redoubt) would be by-passed and dealt with at leisure once the new line was established. This first phase of the attack was scheduled to take thirty minutes. The

A group of Germans pose in a part of their extremely well constructed trenches

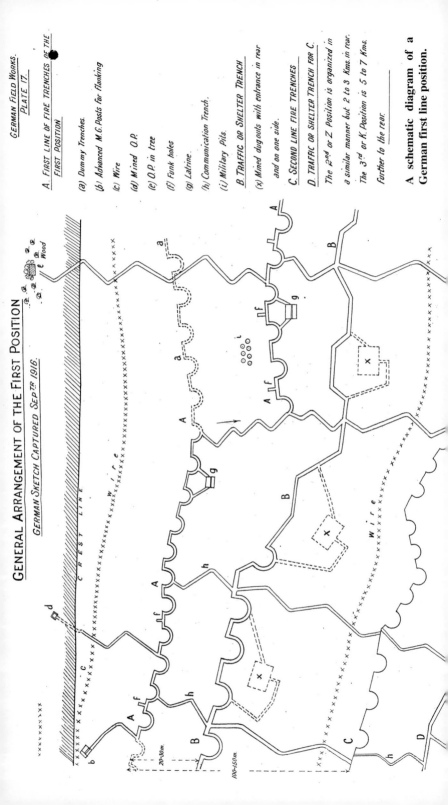

GERMAN FIELD WORKS.
PLATE 17.

GENERAL ARRANGEMENT OF THE FIRST POSITION

GERMAN SKETCH CAPTURED SEPTR 1916.

A. FIRST LINE OF FIRE TRENCHES OF THE FIRST POSITION

(a) *Dummy Trenches.*

(b) *Advanced M.G. Posts for flanking*

(c) *Wire.*

(d) *Mined O.P.*

(e) *O.P. in tree*

(f) *Funk holes*

(g) *Latrine.*

(h) *Communication Trench.*

(i) *Military Pits.*

B. TRAFFIC OR SHELTER TRENCH

(x) *Mined dugouts with entrance in rear and on one side.*

C. SECOND LINE FIRE TRENCHES

D. TRAFFIC OR SHELTER TRENCH FOR C.

The 2nd or Z Position is organized in a similar manner but 2 to 3 Kms. in rear. The 3rd or K. Position is 5 to 7 Kms. further to the rear.

A schematic diagram of a German first line position.

capture of the village and its related defences, now to the west of the British line, would take place some three hours later, after the position had been softened up by the concentration of artillery. This part of the plan reveals one of the great weaknesses of the assault - the lack of time for preparation.

The Gommecourt sector had been held, almost on a 'live and let live' basis, by the 37th Division. The German defenders opposite added up to the equivalent of a new style German division, that is a force of nine battalions. The lack of manpower on the British side, and the lack of tunnellers (specialist tunnelling companies were heavily concentrated on winning the mining fight in the Salient, on Messines Ridge and Vimy Ridge, as well as the major battlefront to the south of Gommecourt) meant that mining operations could not be carried out - operations which would have been particularly efficacious against the deep dugout and redoubt defences to be found on the western edge of Gommecourt.

The problems confronting the two divisions facing the Germans were compounded by two other factors. The first of these related to the distance across which they had to advance to get to the German line - up to half a mile in front of the 56th Division and a quarter of a mile or so in front of the 46th. A further problem lay in the acute shortage of labour which was required to improve the battlefield infrastructure behind the lines and to work on new communication trenches, Russian saps and new jumping off trenches. There was nothing that could be done to avoid the overworking of the men involved, either in these routine tasks or in the preparations over ground mapped out to look like the Gommecourt defences to the rear. The very poor weather at the end of June meant that hardly anyone, particularly on the 46th Division front, which was wet, soggy and poorly drained, managed to get an undisturbed night's rest in the days leading up to the attack.

The outlook was not good. VII Corps were to launch an attack whose success was not considered vital, against well prepared defences and a strong garrison, over open ground well defended by German artillery, with troops of varying degrees of experience, whilst the 56th (London) Division had only been formed in February 1916 (although its infantry battalions were all veterans of the war). In addition, the Corps Commander was under instructions to make his preparations as obvious as possible, which he duly did and resulted in the addition of a German division to the Gommecourt defences and certainly to the volume of VII Corps casualties that were endured on 1 July.

The Germans had the advantage of more artillery - that is if flank fire from Puisieux (to the south east) and Adinfer Wood (to the north east) is included, of heavier calibre and with far more experienced gunners. The British artillery was, by and large, antiquated and almost all of the German heavy guns were beyond the ability of the British to engage in counter-battery work - ie the use of your artillery to destroy that of the enemy. The German barrage at Gommecourt, according to the Official History, was the heaviest on any sector of the battlefront of the Somme on 1 July.

The story of the attack is relatively brief. The 56th Division attack was launched from jumping off trenches that had advanced the British line several hundred yards and were constructed overnight - three thousand yards of trench - on the night of 26/27 May. Attempts to bring this line closer to the Germans (still some four hundred yards and more of No Man's Land remained) had to be abandoned because of the poor weather. The men left their trenches under the cover of a smoke screen and managed to enter the German trenches relatively easily, although suffering heavy casualties from the German barrage that had been pouring on to their assault trenches and the surrounding ground. The Londoners captured the first two lines with little problem and took large numbers of prisoners; however the barrage in No Man's Land meant that many of them had to be kept in the German's own deep dugouts and they were released once the British resistance in the line was crushed. The German defence was concentrated in the third line and around Nameless Farm. As the day progressed, and the British troops ran out of bombs and manpower, a situation compounded by the failure of the 46th Division, the circumstances of the initial waves of troops became increasingly desperate. The barrage was so fierce that reinforcements found it quite impossible to move across the exposed ground, whilst large numbers of German counter attack troops moved in. By the evening the last men in the German lines had returned to their jumping off point; the division had suffered just under 4400

See map on page 16

Gommecourt – the battlefield. Compare with map on page 16.

casualties of whom 1350 were killed.

The story on the 46th (North Midland) Division front was even less encouraging. Although they had less ground to cover to get to the enemy's lines, it was far more muddy than their compatriots on the other side of Gommecourt, who had the advantage of a steeper, and therefore better drained, valley. Similarly, their objectives were limited - establishing a hold in the German line south of the wood, along Oxus communication trench and then a new line established along Fortress Trench and through Little Z back to the old British line. Once a number of strong points were established, the men would go on to join with the 56th along Fill Trench, this being the agreed consolidation line.

Problems along the 46th front were considerable; the ground conditions had made it almost impossible to do anything effective about improving the jumping off arrangements, a situation compounded by the maze of old French trenches, the thick remnants of French wire in No Man's Land and the effective German artillery fire. The ground conditions held up the men, so that the Germans were able to get out of their deep dugouts before the attack lines were much more than halfway across No Man's Land. The smoke screen was effective for half an hour or so, before the wind blew it away - but indeed it was too thick, and numbers of men lost direction and the attack cohesion. The German barrage that came down was extremely effective and severely disrupted the following waves; thus men who were allocated to clear the German dugouts as the first wave went through rarely made it to the German lines. The enemy were thus able to emerge from the protective cover and man the parapet and parados, thereby cutting off those who had got through whilst at the same time able to fend off any reinforcements that had made it through the storm of flying iron that was No Man's Land. To add to the problems of those trying to support the first was the highly effective enfilade machine gun fire from The Z, a salient from the German line.

The left of the 46th Division attack was launched by 139 Brigade, consisting of men from the Sherwood Foresters. There the first two battalions, the attacking waves, broke into the German line, but not without suffering considerable casualties, and suffering the same fate as the lead waves in 137 Brigade from Germans in deep dugouts who had been passed over in the initial assault. The great problem of command for most of the Great War is amply illustrated in this attack by 139 Brigade, typical of the frustration which no amount of planning seemed to be able to overcome.

'Touch with the leading lines was completely lost: the ample means of visual and mechanical communication arranged - telephone, flags, lamps, discs, shutters, pigeons, flares and rockets - all broke down owing to casualties, and no runner could get through. The only signal that came from the front was the lighting of two flares in the second German trench, reported at 11 am from the air.'

The great lesson learned from this set-piece attack on the Somme was the danger of the lack of flexibility in planning, again all too vividly and disastrously revealed here. Men were slow to appreciate changed circumstances and changed orders, radically altering their original tasks on the battlefield. Clogged communication trenches, shortage of munitions (and in particular some bombs) and the difficulty of reorganising under such exposed conditions all served to make attempts to retrieve the situation doomed to failure; planned counter attacks had to be postponed and postponed and then failed to occur because of key personnel becoming casualties and a general air of chaos in the maelstrom that was the front line area. The Division suffered 2500 casualties of whom 850 were killed; the fewest suffered by any British division that was fully committed on the day. The consequence of the day's action was devastating for many men in the Division; it also cost their commander his job. Major-General the Honourable EJ Montagu-Stuart-Wortley was the only divisional commander dismissed as a consequence of his formation's performance. Whilst a court of inquiry on his division's attack was still sitting, he was ordered home by Allenby in the early hours of 5 July. He went on to command the 65th Division in the UK and Ireland, until that was disbanded in March 1918.

Major-General The Honourable E J Montagu-Stuart-Wortley

This is the simple framework of the attack at Gommecourt. The fact that all the units involved in the attack were from the Territorial Force means that there are a good number of battalion histories available, as the Territorials tended to have a more concerned view of their exploits and experiences and often greater financial resources to subsidise the cost of publication. It is thus quite straightforward to put together an account of the experiences of the men and their battalions on that fateful day in July 1916.

Chapter One

THE 56TH DIVISION AREA BEFORE THE BATTLE

One of the finest autobiographical accounts of the Great War, *Four Years on the Western Front*, was published in 1922 and republished ten years or so ago by the London Stamp Exchange (Naval and Military Press) in one of their series of most useful reprints. Its author was anonymous in the first edition, but was later identified as Aubrey Smith. He joined the London Rifle Brigade in August 1914, went to France in January 1915 and in September 1915 joined the transport section. He served throughout the war and by the armistice had won the MM (August 1917) and a Bar in November 1918. His is a literate, detailed and fascinating account of a Territorial battalion in the Great War and is strongly recommended.

See maps on pages 16, 28, 127,136

Smith describes the days before the battle and the problems of bringing supplies to the front, an unglamorous aspect of war and one which is all too frequently ignored in favour of the 'glamour' of the events in and around the front line.

The Brigade horse lines were established on 21 May at Bayencourt, a village to the north west of Sailly au Bois, itself about a mile to the west of Hebuterne. Smith and his companions had reached the spot after an overnight stay at St Amand. The billet allocated was far from satisfactory; it

> 'roused roars of merriment when we were introduced to it. It was a dilapidated barn with little roof, collapsing sides and an earth floor, the latter being full of ruts and holes. (One) said he would rather sleep in a midden [a very ripe manure heap].'

Before they could establish a bivvy (bivouac, constructed essentially of

Road below Bayencourt along which Aubrey Smith made his way to Hebuterne. It became known as Happy Valley.

The new field kitchen filled with removable ovens. One hundred meals of soup, joints, vegetables, tea etc., could be served. Very little coal was required as the fire was kept going with wood or dry refuse found on the field. TAYLOR LIBRARY

groundsheets and whatever came to hand to provide shelter), he and a friend were instructed to take the company cookers up to Hebuterne with the ration convoy.

> *'This was a peculiar part of the front, there could be no doubt of that! The companies were to have their four cookers brought up and dumped in Hebuterne, where hot meals would be provided for the men in the trenches some two hundred yards away. Rumour said that when the French were on this front, there was such a complete truce that they and the Germans used to send orderlies in turn to use a pump in No Man's Land.'*

The route that Smith followed can be easily followed to-day. It was not a straightforward drive.

> *'The convoy started off seemingly in the wrong direction, but its purpose was to work round in a semicircle on to the Hebuterne road, instead of passing along the sky-line on the more direct route. The way was narrow and the little lane was bounded by hedges and trees, so that it was difficult in places for*

Large mortars nicknamed Toffee apples.

limbers coming in opposite directions to pass us. Brakesmen toiled and perspired in a vain endeavour to regulate the brakes to the satisfaction of the drivers as we passed down the decline through the outskirts of the straggling place; drivers held their horses back, but could not help occasionally nearly decapitating the brakesman of the limber in front, as the pole shot forward too far.'

Just outside the village they passed a huge ammunition dump hidden under a canvas roof, and this was the first time he had sight of 'toffee apples', large mortars the size of small footballs attached to long metal poles.

'Halfway to our destination, or rather more, perhaps, our little country road led us into a village with scarcely any sign of damage - Sailly au Bois - lying directly behind Hebuterne and about one and a half miles from the trenches. Directly we emerged from the trees on the far side we should be under observation, so the convoy had to wait with many other limbers until it was dark before we could pass that spot.'

The village was beginning to fill with the heavy artillery that was to be used in the forthcoming battle. Finally the police allowed them to proceed, one limber at a time with a hundred yard interval between each.

'..emerging from the wooded valley we made out way individually across the Hebuterne plain, which was about a mile of rough moor and grassland separating one village from the other. At the entrance to Hebuterne, I came to a tunnel of trees which made it so dark momentarily that I could not see a yard in front or to either side of me - I simply left it to the horses to carry on, which they did as well as could be expected under the circumstance. They chose the correct road out of five turnings which were indistinguishable to me and kept to the centre of the road to avoid branches hitting me in the face!' [This crossroads is the one which leads to, amongst other places, Hebuterne Military Cemetery.]

He proceeded from here into the centre of Hebuterne, turning right at

27

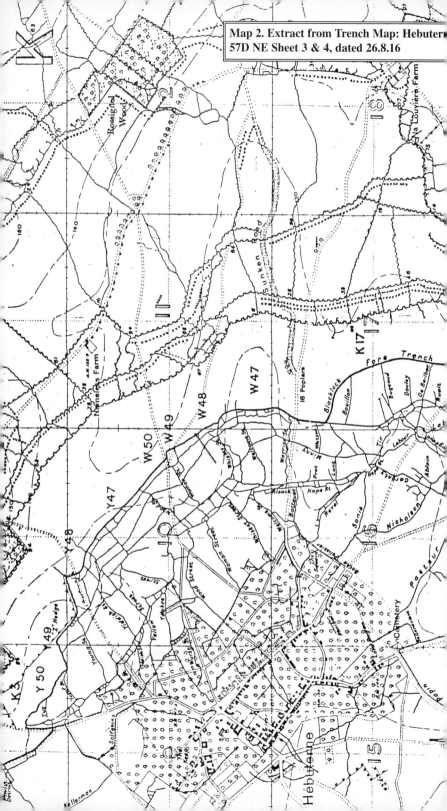

**Map 2. Extract from Trench Map: Hebuter
57D NE Sheet 3 & 4, dated 26.8.16**

the pond, which has now been removed, and being led up the main street towards the church, being warned at the same time that the Germans intermittently let loose with machine gun along the road.

Returning to Bayencourt, Smith discovered that he was not a natural camper, as he caused chaos in the confines of the bivvy. They soon discovered that they were not alone, as a battery of 9.2 inch howitzers, newly arrived from England, were established close by, silent weapons, not opening fire until much closer to the battle so as to avoid German counter battery work, and which were aimed at the woods around Gommecourt.

'The revelation of these hidden guns, however, acted like magic upon our spirits. The visual proof that we had something 'up our sleeves' - a surprise in the shape of a really heavy bombardment - was the very thing that we had wished for among all the vague rumours of an offensive that had been passed around.'

There were plenty of problems for the transport section; the village only had one completely inadequate well, the troughs were at Coigneux, which meant that their horses had to be taken there three times a day and then had to compete with the hundreds of other horses from the various units who also had the same problems. The transport was in frequent demand for a whole variety of tasks and the men had to be up each day at 5.30 am.

On 23 May he opted to return from Hebuterne on the more direct route, using the Souastre road from Sailly au Bois; just outside Bayencourt he found eight new gun pits dug alongside the road so that its use would be out of the question when they were firing. An

The church in Hebuterne in the early stages of its destruction.

The grassed area is the site of the village pond in Hebuterne.

attempted short cut to his billet led to him being held up by a newly arrived gun team.

> *'I distinguished something looming up out of the darkness just before me, impeding my progress. My horses pricked up their ears and stopped short. Ahead of me lamps were being flashed, revealing a huge gun with a tractor in front of it, one wheel being sunk in the ditch...The officer came up and said I should be able to get by presently; he asked me if there was any danger in flashing torches about as he had not been in the firing line before; none of his men had, he said, and they had been hurried out here with their training only half-finished...How the hell the army expected etc etc.'*

Although the incident is amusing enough - probably not, however, at the time - it underlines one of the key features of the 1916 Battle of the Somme: the inexperience of so many of the men. It is not that they had not spent a long time training or even in the army, but rather had a shortage of equipment (in this case guns) or of actual battle experience, factors which objectively makes it understandable why senior officers had doubts about the wisdom of such a major offensive at this stage and goes some way to explaining the tactics adopted on 1 July.

Hebuterne was a billeting area for those serving in the trenches. The Keep, just to the east of the present military cemetery, was one of the billets, saved from German observation partly by the lie of the ground, partly by the bulk of the village to the east. The period after the construction of the new line in late May was a difficult one, as trenches, in particular communication trenches, were very narrow; and the Germans took advantage of the newness and underdeveloped nature of the position by putting it under frequent *minenwerfer* (mortar) and artillery fire. So narrow were the communication trenches at this stage that they could not take a stretcher, and one soldier wounded in the head had to undergo a five hour carry by stretcher bearers, using nothing more than sandbags under his arms and knees, to get him out to an aid post in Hebuterne.

The Rangers were billeted in Souastre much of the time in June. Tasks included burying the divisional cable (phone) line from Sailly to Hebuterne. The Divisional concert party, the 'Bow Bells' put on shows in a barn in the village, with *My Old Kentucky Home* being a particularly popular number.

> *Even now when a barrel-organ comes round and plays that song beneath the windows of any 1916 member of the 56th Division, his memory will travel quickly back to the old barn at Souastre, the smoke from pipes rising on the warm air, and the laughing faces of his old pals round him; he will smile at the recollection of that pleasant interlude in a life of toil and danger, but he will sigh when he realises how many of those laughing companions have since 'gone west'. 'And then to bed.' as Pepys would say, or rather, blankets on the floor of a barn, and sleep to the hammering of a machine gun two miles away.*

Patrols were common during the period, whilst German snipers and motar crews were active - spots like Lone Tree were particularly dangerous. One wag had placed a notice just where the sunken road

Men of the R. Berkshire Regiment in a front line trench. Hebuterne, August 1915. TAYLOR LIBRARY

Troops rehearsing a battle. Note the use of smoke. TAYLOR LIBRARY

met the support line (just as the sunken road begins to the east of Hebuterne, on the road to Bucquoy), *'If you don't want to become a, landowner in France, keep well down whilst crossing the sunken road'*.

The Division carried out its rehearsals over a number of days between 22nd and 26th June in the peaceful calm of Halloy, a village a few kilometres east of Doullens and well away from the battlefield; this included practices at all levels over replica trenches, culminating in a full dress rehearsal involving all the staffs up to Corps, aircraft and smoke.[1] The history of the QVRs notes of these rehearsals,

> *The preparations for the attack were the best rehearsed of any that the QVR did. Instead of, as often occurred afterwards, hardly anyone knowing anything of the work to be done, every single man in the battalion knew all about the attack and what was expected of him.*

The QVR also had time to relax.

> *A memorable dinner took place at Halloy when about forty officers assembled in a big hut on the evening of June 23rd. It was a sort of send-off for the Great Push which it was expected would take place within a day or two. Menu cards were passed round and autographed by all present. Contrary to mess custom a few speeches were made wishing success to the battalion in the approaching battle and altogether a very pleasant evening was spent. Sixteen of the signatories of the menus figured in the casualty list for July 1st, and the cards are now highly prized by the fortunate survivors as a melancholy souvenir of their former companions.*

Meanwhile, in the background, preparations continued for what would result in the almost continuous rumbling of the guns as the artillery relentlessly bombarded the German lines preparatory to the great attack.

1. *The Rangers' Historical Records* ed Captain AV Wheeler-Houlan and Captain GMG Wyatt. Chenies Street n.d.

Chapter Two

THE ATTACK OF THE 56TH DIVISION

The preparations for the attack were a stupendous exercise in the construction of an infrastructure to sustain and support a massive offensive designed to last for several months (albeit not designed to sit in more or less the start off area for several months) in an area which was a quiet rural backwater where the most exciting recent developments in this regard had been the construction of a number of light railways to facilitate the development of the sugar beet industry.

Stores had to be made available and secured in deep dugouts - these for food, water and engineering material, but also for dressing stations, for sheltering troops and for protecting ammunition stocks. The whole trench system had to be upgraded and massively extended. Dumps had to be established (and roads for their supply repaired or created); whilst miles of railway line of different gauges had to be laid along with water mains, over a hundred pumping stations were installed and innumerable wells were dug. All of this was done with the very considerable aid of the men of the infantry battalions, and was completed over a very limited period of time - a matter of four months. This obviously restricted the amount of time that could be spent in practising for the attack, but practice trenches were constructed and time given to going over the details of the attack, the identification of the features on the ground (such as they were), the German trench system and procedures to be followed during the attack.

Preparing trench mortar ammunition for the trenches. TAYLOR LIBRARY

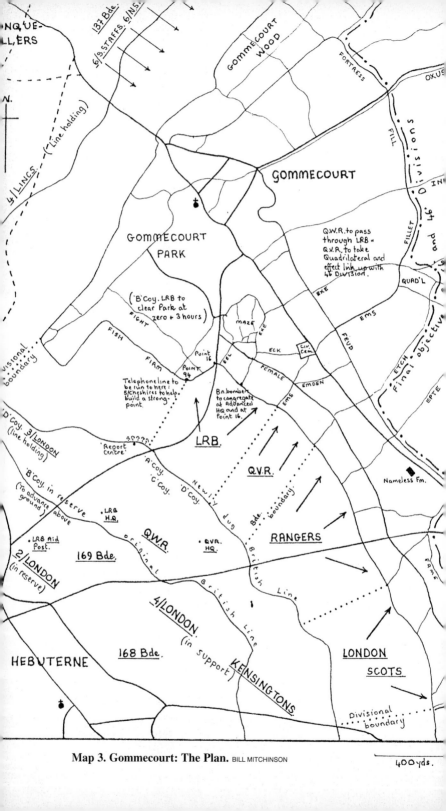

Map 3. Gommecourt: The Plan. BILL MITCHINSON

400 yds.

The small but powerful tractor is easily pulling a heavy gun which would otherwise require a team of horses.

In a paragraph I have attempted to describe what was necessary before the battle began, and it really gives but a poor impression of the frenetic activity that was the characteristic of the Somme battle area in the spring and early summer of 1916. It is hardly surprising that, in the light of all of this, there was a feeling of apprehensive confidence amongst many of those taking part.

The right attack: 168 Brigade.

The London Scottish (14/London Regiment) were on the extreme right of the attack, with the Kensingtons in support; the Rangers were to the left, with 4/London in support. They had with them a company of 5/Cheshires, the Pioneer battalion for the division, whose task it was to assist with creating blocks in the German defence system in order to make the newly captured position tenable.

The plan of the brigade was to make a half wheel to the right and then to capture the strong point round about Farm and Farmer trenches, and establish other strong points at Elbe and Et, south east of Nameless

56th Division attack: the front line battalions.

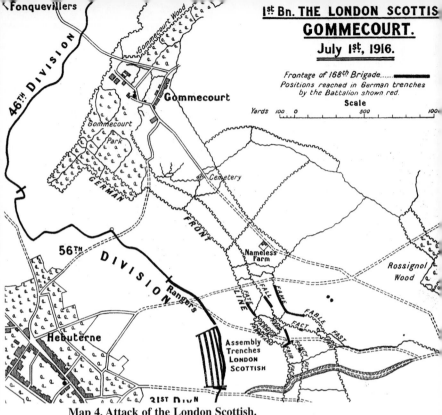

Fonquevillers

1st Bn. THE LONDON SCOTTIS
GOMMECOURT.
July 1st, 1916.

Frontage of 168th Brigade......■■■■■
Positions reached in German trenches
by the Battalion shown red.
Scale
Yards 100 0   500   100

46TH DIVISION

Gommecourt Wood

Gommecourt

Gommecourt Park

GERMAN

Cemetery

FRONT

56TH

DIVISION

Rangers

Nameless Farm

Rossignol Wood

LINE

EPTE

FELON

FABLE

FACT

FANCY

FAST

FAIR

Hebuterne

Assembly
Trenches
LONDON
SCOTTISH

21ST DIVN

Map 4. Attack of the London Scottish.

Farm, and the junction of Felon and Epte. The view that lay in front of
the men of the 56th Division was recalled by John Masefield's
masterly *The Old Front Line*, published in 1917.

> *All the country there is gentler and less decided than in the
> southern parts of the battlefield. Hebuterne stands on a plateau
> top; to the east of it there is a gentle dip down to a shallow
> hollow or valley; to the east of this again there is a gentle rise to
> higher ground, on which the village of Gommecourt stood...*

> *Seen from our front line at Hebuterne, Gommecourt is little
> more than a few red brick buildings, standing in woodland on a
> rise of ground. Wood hides the village to the north, the west and
> the south-west. A big spur of woodland, known as Gommecourt
> Park, thrusts out boldly from the village towards the plateau on
> which the English lines stood. This spur, strongly fortified by the
> enemy, made the greater part of the salient in the enemy lines.
> The landscape away from the wood is not in any way remarkable,
> except that it is open, and gentle and on a generous scale.
> Looking north from our position at Hebuterne there is the snout
> of the woodland salient; looking south there is the green shallow*

shelving hollow or valley which made the No Man's Land for rather more than a mile.

It is very much the same view today.

Note that all German stretches of Front Line trench system (ie three lines) in the Gommecourt sector were given names beginning with the letter F; and that these trenches, from south to north, went in alphabetical order thereafter - ie from Face in the south, on 56th Division front, to Fuss in the north on the 46th Division Front. Communication Trenches (CTs) followed a similar system, beginning with the letter E on the 56th Division and the letter O on the 46th Division's. The one exception was the trench known as Maze, just to the east of Gommecourt Park and south of the Kern (Maze) Redoubt.

The attack was prefaced by a hurricane bombardment (following the steady, softening-up artillery attack that had been going on for seven days) and the release of a smoke screen; to prevent the Germans from knowing that this was part of the attack, smoke had been released periodically during the previous days' bombardments. This ruse was in vain, as the Germans were all too well aware of when the attack was to come. The smoke was thicker than it had been in the practice sessions, and this led to confusion; thus the right company's (A) lead platoon lost direction and ended up going off well to the right of its axis, followed by another. The problem for A Company was that their part of the line bent away from the German line, and thus they had to make a slight swing to the left in order to attain their target. The other companies stretched to their left in the order C, B and D.

London Scottish

The two platoons lost in the smoke were effectively destroyed before they could recover from their mistake, and only a few men actually made it to the German wire. The two following platoons, for the most part, did get to the German front line, having crossed some three hundred yards of No Man's Land, but were confronted by German wire which had been largely untouched by the bombardment. However, they came across a gap in the wire that had been created for the German patrols, and were thus able to enter the front line with comparative ease at the junction of Fair and Farmyard; this relatively small garrison was an example of the German defence tactics, which involved holding the front line positions lightly, saving their men from the bombardment and using them in due course to counter-attack.

B Company was more successful, advancing through smoke that was so thick that the men could see neither of the neighbouring companies, through the utterly destroyed German wire and over a German trench that was battered beyond recognition. It reached its

View from near the German second line, near Rossignol Wood.

objective, Fame, without difficulty, and extended its line leftwards, all the time coming under German fire from their second line. C Company for the most part had a similar success, although they had to deal with a party of Germans that emerged from their deep dugouts after the first wave had passed over. They established themselves in Farmyard and Farmer and moved on to the third German trench of the front line position, Farm - or so they thought. In fact the company had failed to find its initial objective because of the destruction wrought by the seven days of bombardment and had overshot into Fable.

Meanwhile A Company had tried to form blocks on the extreme right of the attack, in Fancy and Fair, as the whole operation was liable to enfilade fire from German snipers, whilst strong parties of German bombers were trying to unravel this 'refused' flank.

The acting commander of C Company, having sent back wounded,

The two men in the centre of this photograph are engaged in cleaning a Lewis gun. Above their heads is a foghorn, for use in case of a gas attack.

GOMMECOURT PARK   GOMMECOURT   GOMMECOURT WOOD

including his company commander, took half his remaining force to probe forward to what he thought would be Fable. Instead he found himself, as the view cleared, well down the slope and vulnerable to fire from all sorts of direction, most notably from the high ground on the opposite side of the valley. The company withdrew back to Fable. The company was reduced to about sixty effectives, one officer and no senior NCOs within twenty five minutes of setting off from their trenches.

D Company suffered a disaster when almost an entire platoon was destroyed by shell fire in the assembly trenches. When they did get to the Front Line they found the German wire uncut and the trench manned by a resolute, if small, garrison. This force was eventually overcome, but progress was always difficult, especially as the left flank, adjacent to the Rangers, was not secured, and thus the company came under fire from the side as well as the front. It was a much reduced company that eventually fought its way to the third trench line.

The situation was quite dire. By 8 am the Germans were able to turn their entire attention to the 56th Division front; the companies were all in very reduced states and the ferocious German barrage in No Man's Land ensured that it was impractical to obtain reinforcements or supplies, particularly of bombs, which were vital at this stage. The Germans were massing themselves for a counter attack in a trench system that ran along or just above the Gommecourt-Puisieux road (Namless Road). Two companies were holding Fame and the left part of Fable; the few men remaining in D Company were holding the eastern part of Fall, whilst A was desperately trying to hold the Germans on the right. The whole position, in shattered trenches, was vulnerable to fire from the German trenches which made maximum use of the high ground which ran from the northern tip of Rossignol Wood in to the eastern part of Gommecourt.

By 9 am the Rangers had had to give ground on their right, making the London Scottish position increasingly untenable, and shortly afterwards Major Lindsay, who commanded, withdrew the remnants to Farm and Fall.

Attempts by the Kensingtons to come to their support came to very little; only the odd box of ammunition and a number of individuals making it through the intense barrage and sniper fire. The Rangers had, by about 3 pm, been completely cleared from the German trenches, Major Lindsay had been killed, whilst the Germans brought up field batteries that took up position on the slope to the south east of Rossignol Wood and started pounding the battered defenders with enfilade fire.

At 4 pm the commander, Captain Sparks, sent the following message to battalion headquarters:

I am faced with this position.

I have collected all bombs and SAA (small arms ammunition) from casualties. Every one has been used.

I am faced with three alternatives:

a. To stay here with such of my men as are alive and be killed

b. To surrender to the enemy

c. To withdraw such of my men as I can.

Either of these first two alternatives is distasteful to me. I propose to adopt the latter.

The men gradually withdrew into Farmyard from the east end of Farm and then they made use of an unfinished German sap which ran out towards the British line. A small group consisting of Sparks, another officer and several NCOs covered the departure of the rest; two of the former were killed trying to get back to the British lines. Sparks took cover in a shell hole and got back to the British line during the night, to be met by an incredulous commanding officer, Lieutenant-Colonel Green, who had had detailed reports of his death.

Returning to Gommecourt as a Colonel, in 1917, Sparks revisited the site of the battle; and arranged for a cross to be erected made from gun timbers taken from the battlefield with an inscription on a plate of brass metal also found on the battlefield. It no longer exists.

The remnants of the battalion gathered at the point where the old British Front Line (ie that of before late May 1916) met the Hebuterne

Routing Germans from dug-outs.

to Puisieux road; they had lost some seventy percent out of the 856 men who had gone into action - perhaps most extraordinary of all was the fact that all of the stretcher bearers survived almost undamaged and none was unable to answer the roll call at this spot.[1]

In 1980 A. Stuart Dolden published his memoirs of his time with the London Scottish. Despite its pejorative title, *Cannon Fodder*, it is not an anti general diatribe, and is an interesting account of a soldier's life on the Western Front of over three years of the war. As was usual for a number of units within the London Regiment, recruits to the ranks were likely to be of the professional classes; and he was no exception, being a recently qualified solicitor; in any case, you had to pay a pound to join the Scottish - and this was true even in November 1914! For most of his war he was a company cook, which was not without its hazards, as his Quartermaster used to boast to all other quartermasters that he could get his cookers further forward than any other. His contribution to 1 July was confined to bringing the cookers up to Bayencourt and then moving into Hebuterne at about 4 pm to provide the survivors with tea. In the post 1 July period, when the company was so short of men, he got seconded back to his platoon and noted the recovery of a wounded Fusilier from No Man's Land by a London Scottish patrol - thirteen days after the battle, during which period he could only remember two dawns. He survived and was able to attend a post war London Scottish reunion as a guest of his rescuer.

To the rear of the London Scottish were the men of the Kensingtons, the 13th London Regiment. Their task was entirely one of support to the Scottish, with the exception of a reinforced A Company, whose task **Kensingtons** it was to dig a new trench from the British line to the captured German trenches, facing south to act as part of the new line; and a number of platoons from Headquarters and B Company, whose task it was to clean up the German dugouts crossed by the Scottish by a liberal use of bombs. This latter group was to follow close on to the rear of the Scottish and to come under its command. The remainder of B Company was to act as carrying parties, whilst the rest of the battalion, C and D Companies, were to take the place of the Scottish in the British trenches as a reserve.

In fact A Company, which had been instructed not to dig the trench until it was so instructed, had little to do, so switched its attention to supporting the Scottish with ammunition and bombs. The companies in the old British line, which had been hastily dug and was devoid of even half decent shelters, suffered terribly from the German defensive

Site of Nameless Farm looking towards Hebuterne and the attack of Queen Victoria's Rifles and the London Scottish. See page 35.

† GOMMECOURT No 2

SUNKEN ROAD

EBUTERNE - PUISIEUX ROAD

barrage that raked No Man's Land. The conditions were atrocious, as was revealed by the forward commander, Major CC Dickens, in various messages which he sent to battalion headquarters:

1.10 pm. Shelling fearful. Trench practically untenable, full of dead and wounded. Very few men indeed left. Must have instructions and assistance.

1.48 pm. Sap absolutely impassable owing to shell fire. Every party that enters it is knocked out at once. Captain Ware has been wounded somewhere there. I have just crawled to the end of it with Scottish machine gun party. Could not find him. [His body was never identified, and he is commemorated on the Thiepval Memorial.] *One of Scottish had his hand blown off. Our front line is in an awful state. Two more men killed and one wounded. Estimate casualties to A and C Companies at least 25 killed and 5 wounded. Impossible to man large lengths of our front line. Digging quite out of the question and position of the Scottish serious.*

2.12 pm. I have as far as I can find only 13 left besides myself. Trenches unrecognisable. Quite impossible to hold. Bombardment fearful for last two hours. I am the only officer left. Please send instructions.

Major Dickens survived this battle; he was killed in an attack on Ginchy, to the south of the Somme battlefield, on 9 September, and has a well known and unique commemoration.

The Kensingtons remained in the line until nightfall, when they were relieved by 8/Middlesex, which had been brought up to Souastre during the battle as part of the reserve. The weary residue of the battalion spent the night in the open in the old French trenches near Sailly au Bois, having lost 16 officers and 300 other ranks out of its battle strength of 23 officers and 592 other ranks; they were back in the line on 2 July in the Fonquevillers sector.[2]

A soldier who served with the battalion until April 1918, when he was severely wounded in the arm and was subsequently discharged, was John F Tucker, who wrote his memoirs in 1978 under the title *Johnny Get Your Gun*. On arriving at Souastre he was detailed to the transport section, but it was his talents as a sign writer that enabled him to contribute to the battle on 1 July. To assist the artillery observers and the contact aircraft of the Royal Flying Corps, as well as the infantry, the attacking troops were issued with large trench signs painted with the appropriate name to be erected as the relevant trenches were captured. He recalled that the Quartermaster, a veteran of the South

African war, burst into tears when he saw all that was left of the battalion on its return from the attack. He was also responsible for painting and helping to erect the cross and railing marking the grave of Major Dickens; killed in September 1916 the memorial was erected when the battalion returned to the vicinity the following year.

To the left of the London Scottish were the Rangers (12/London Regiment).They had got into their position by 3.40 am from their billets in Bayencourt, taking a circuitous route on the Blue Track via Sailly and coming into Hebuterne from the southern outskirts. Troops were kept off the roads as much as possible, leaving this to wheeled traffic; it also made the infantry less vulnerable to the periodic 'hates' - bursts of shell fire by the German artillery on particularly likely spots for targets.

Their position was from Woman Street (a communication trench) on the right to a point about fifty yards to the left of Wood Street, with companies from right to left in alphabetical order, starting with A, in four waves with a seventy yard interval between them. With the exception of their next door neighbours, the QVR (Queen Victoria's Rifles), they had the furthest stretch of No Man's Land to cross of any battalion in either of the two divisions engaged in the attack on Gommecourt. It had a terrible time.

John Masefield described the German position at Gommecourt in his introduction to Edward Liveing's *Attack on the Somme*.

Germans constructing a reinforced shelter. TAYLOR LIBRARY

The position is immensly strong in itself, with a perfect glacis and field of fire. Every invention of modern defensive war helped to make it stronger. In front of it was the usual system of barbed wire stretched on iron supports over a width of fifty yards. Behind the wire was the system of the First Enemy Main Line, from which many communication trenches ran to the central fortress of the Salient known as the Kern Redoubt and to the Support or Guard Line. This First Line is a great and deep trench of immense strength...at intervals it is strengthened with small forts or sentry-boxes of concrete built into the parapet [the front of a trench]. *Great and deep dugouts lie below it. At the mouth of some of these one may see giant-legged periscopes by which men sheltered in the dugout shafts could watch for the coming of an attack...Though the wire was formidable and the trench immense, the real defences of the position were artillery and machine guns...The enemy had not less than a dozen machine guns in and in front of the Kern Redoubt. Some of these were cunningly hidden in pits, tunnels and shelters in (or even outside) the obstacle of the wire at the salient, so they could enfilade the No Man's Land or shoot an attacking party in the back after it had passed.[3]*

The Rangers' task was to cross 400 yards or so of No Man's Land and to consolidate a position from Fame on the right along a portion of Elbe (a communication trench), then along the length of Felon to its junction with Epte, that is a frontage of about 560 yards and which would also include the capture of the strongly defended Nameless Farm.

The battalion suffered extremely heavily in crossing No Man's Land, partly in consequence of the murderous German fire, but largely because the German wire seemed to have suffered minimal damage from the artillery barrage and was still a major obstacle. It took A Company two hours to bomb its way into Fall and then, with the assistance of men from the London Scottish, held a part of Fame and the communication trench (Elbe) to it until about 3 pm. B Company had suffered painfully from the German bombardment before they even went over the top, were held up by German wire and only a few actually got through into the German position. All but one of the officers of this company were seriously wounded before they even reached the German wire. C Company managed to break through into the German line, despite similar problems with uncut wire, but the survivors then found themselves faced with Nameless Farm and made no headway, despite reinforcements from 4/London Regiment. The survivors were forced to make their way back to their original line. D Company had a similarly miserable experience, where the attack failed before the uncut German wire. Some men got through, and were consolidating a position at about 10 am, but nothing more was seen or heard of them. This party was joined with stragglers from the QVRs, but were forced back by German attacks which were launched in force from about noon onwards and eventually joined up with the remnants of A Company. Most of these retired back to the British lines at about 3 pm, except for a small group that got detached from the London Scottish and were eventually captured by the Germans.

Edward Liveing wrote a most vivid account of the action. From the internal evidence it would seem that he was an officer of B Company. He describes the approach into the trenches from the billets; collecting various items of trench stores from difficult-to-find dumps, avoiding stray shrapnel along the main street, known as Boulevard and finally entering a communication trench.

> *It was, as always, a relief to enter the recesses of Wood Street without having anyone hit. We clattered along the brick-floored trench, whose walls were overhung with the dewy grass and flowers of the orchard - that wonderful orchard whose aroma had survived the horror and desolation of two years' warfare,*

See maps on pages 28, 127

One of John Macefield's 'small forts'.

and seemed now only to be intensified to a softer fragrance by the night air.

From here he moved along Cross Street and then into Woman Street, past Brigade Headquarters (where the Brigade Major was relieved to hear of his company's presence) and from there on to New Woman Street and out to the point where this trench met the sunken road, not far from Lone Tree and nowadays approximately on the site of Gommecourt British Cemetery No. 2. Whilst sorting out his sections he notes that he was picked out by a German searchlight from the direction of Serre. He slept fitfully during the night and the dawn came.

There was the freshness and splendour of a summer morning over everything. In fact, as one man said, it felt more as if we were going to start off for a picnic than a battle.

Perhaps the joys of the summer's morning made up for the horrors that he had already graphically described. Certainly any illusion of rural bliss was soon rudely shattered by the final bombardment.

I had an excessive desire for the time to come when I should go 'over the top', when I should be free at last from the noise of the bombardment, free from the prison of my trench, free to walk across that patch of No Man's Land and opposing trenches till I got to my objective, or, if I did not go that far, to have my fate decided for better or for worse. I experienced, too, moments of intense fear during close bombardment.

He continues in this vein, with his disbelief and churning mind awakened by the reality of the call for stretcher bearers. His platoon was in the third wave, due to set off at 7.30 and forty five seconds. He got over the trench and swung his rifle to start his platoon's part in the battle. It is worth noting here that a lot of officers took rifles with them rather than their pistols - partly to make themselves less conspicuous, partly because the pistol was - indeed is - of rather limited military practicability. Later in the war many offices wore other ranks uniform, and badges of rank were moved from cuffs to the epaulettes to make officers a less obvious target to German snipers.

The scene that met my eyes as I stood on the parapet of our trench for one second is almost indescribable. Just in front the ground was pitted by innumerable shell holes. More holes opened suddenly every now and then. Here and there a few bodies lay about...Everything stood still for a second, as a panorama painted with three colours - the white of the smoke, the red of the shrapnel and blood, the green of the grass.

46

He advanced, nervousness gone, as in a dream and then got up to the German wire. Soon afterwards he was wounded in the hip, though at first he thought he had been scalded by boiling water, perhaps coming from water in a shell hole that had been boiled by a bursting shell. After being assisted by a sergeant he crawled back to the line,

> I crawled very slowly at first. Little holes opened in the ground on either side of me, and I understood that I was under the fire of a machine gun.

He fell into the sunken road, then crawled over the embankment on the other side - the road was dangerous, as the Germans had a machine gun fixed on it, which killed many of those who came into it. After crawling around, unsure of his whereabouts, he found himself at the head of the communication trench, New Woman Street (unaware at the time that this was what it was).

> The scene at the head of that communication trench is stamped in a blurred but unforgettable way on my mind. In the remains of a wrecked dugout or emplacement a signaller sat, calmly transmitting messages to Battalion Headquarters. A few bombers were walking along the continuation of the front line. I could distinguish the red grenades on their arms through the smoke.

The book goes on to describe vividly his removal through the various stages of the medical evacuation. The book is a tremendous and moving account of one officer's experience on 1 July; what is more extraordinary is that it was published, in all its vivid detail, in December 1917.[4] Although a very slim volume, it is one of the imaginative reprints that Spa Books has done in recent years in association with Tom Donovan Military Books. This edition includes a

German machine gun team preparing to bring down fire. These teams, right up to the end of the war, were extremely effective.

roll of honour of all of those who were killed in the battalion on 1 July.

At midnight the battalion was relieved and returned to Sailly and the Corps Line, which they occupied at 1.30 am. One officer out of sixteen who went over the top remained; about 200 out of the 745 other ranks. Just as so many of the Pals battalions were to lose their recruiting characteristic as a consequence of 1 July, so also did the membership of many of the Territorial battalions; certainly this was true of the Rangers, which would receive reinforcements with backgrounds unrelated to its tradition.[5]

The left attack: 169 Brigade.

Attack Order No 1 for Queen Victoria's Rifles (9/London Regiment) laid out the objectives of 169 Brigade.

Queen Victoria's Rifles

The task of the 169th Brigade will be carried out in 4 phases.

1st Phase. To capture from left of 168th Brigade along Fell, Fellow, Feud, Cemetery, Eck, Maze, Eel and Fir, and establish three strong points, viz:

See map on page 49

     1. Near Cemetery
     2. At the Maze
     3. At the SE corner of Gommecourt Park

2nd Phase (immediately after 1st). To clear Ems, Etch and capture the Quadrilateral.

3rd Phase (immediately after 2nd). To secure cross trenches at K5a.78, where Indus crosses Fell and Fillet to join hands with 46th Division along Fill and consolidate Fillet, facing East.

4th Phase (to commence three hours after zero). To clear both Gommecourt Village and Park in a NW direction from line Fir-Eel-Maze-Eck-Cemetery.

The battalion had one company in reserve, D, which was positioned in the area of battalion headquarters, which were situated at the junction of Yellow Street and the old Front Line, from which place there were extensive views across the battlefield. The regimental history comments on the creation of a battle surplus, something which all the histories mention. This, the history records, was an innovation and was strictly carried out throughout the army; in the sense that this was to be uniformly imposed, this is true; though the policy had been implemented by individual formations in previous set-piece battles. In the case of the QVRs eight officers and ninety ORs were left out of the battle with the transport. These were mainly specialists such as bombers and Lewis gunners. The principle of the operation was that these men would provide the cadre around which battalions could be

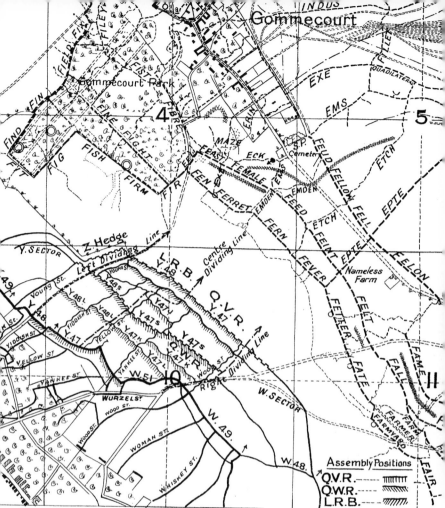

Map 5. Gommecourt, 1 July 1916. 169 Brigade attack.

rebuilt efficiently and relatively quickly.

The events of the day were summarised by the Victoria's commanding officer, Colonel Dickins.

> *For two hours no news whatever was received from the front, all communication, visual and telephonic, having failed. Beyond answering constant appeals from the Brigade for information, we had leisure to observe what was going on. Meanwhile a steady shelling of our trenches was kept up and New Yellow Street (our up CT* [ie only to be used going towards the British line] *from the old front line) was filled up and destroyed for a great length of its course. Two companies of 3/London under*

Major Samuels attempted to dig a CT across No Man's Land, but heavy rifle fire and mg fire completely prevented them. Information was then received - more than an hour old from both Cox and Houghton [company commanders of C and B respectively], *that all their objectives had been quickly taken. This was brought by two plucky runners who returned to our line through the barrage. Thenceforward the day went ill. The stubborn resistance of the enemy, the shortage of bombs, and the impossibility of getting more across to our men on the far side, and lastly the complete failure of the 46th Division's assault on the left and the repulse of the 31st Division on our right* [attacking at Serre], *were the causes of our disastrous reverse at Gommecourt.*

What is interesting about this account is the fact that the battalion commander, despite being far forward, had almost no idea what was going on; he had good views of the battlefield (albeit obscured for some time by the smoke) but he found it almost impossible to know just what was happening. This underlines the problems faced by those commanding formations higher up; if the man on the spot could not tell what was happening, how was the Brigade or Divisional commander to know? How was the artillery to react? This passage is an eloquent exposé of the single greatest problem faced by commanders of the Great War - the practical impossibility of controlling a battle once it had begun by anyone much further from the action than the men on the spot. It was only as technology evolved that things changed - so that by 1918 communications had improved dramatically, though even then they were a pale reflection to those which were available to commanders of the Second World War.

Col. Vernon W F Dickins, DSO, VD

Colonel Dickins wrote an account based on notes taken at the time.

As soon as the assault commenced, the German barrage was opened on to our trenches; though not severe at first, it increased in intensity later. By 9.48 the assaulting companies had reached their objective and occupied it after heavy fighting. [This is the only information he received,

as indicated in the passage above, from the head of the attack]
They did not, however, get in touch with the battalion on the right [ie the Rangers]. *At the same time the third company was consolidating the German second line. The Germans were pressing hard at this time and the shortage of bombs began to be felt. In accordance with the orders as to the fourth phase of the battle, three sections of bombers with battle police from the reserve company were ordered at 9.30 am to join the companies in the German line. Owing, however, to congestion in the communications trenches, this party did not leave until after 10.30. As soon as they left the trench they came under heavy machine gun fire and half the party became casualties immediately. This party was unable to get across No Man's Land, the enemy barrage by this time being intense. At eleven o'clock the shortage of bombs became critical. From 12.30 to 1.30 the German counter-attack increased in force, and the companies were driven back from the third line to the second line. At 2 o'clock the companies were driven back to the German first line. About this time a few wounded men began to reach our lines. At 4.30 orders were received to collect all stragglers in our lines, and hold the assembly trench strongly. From this time until about 7 pm survivors in German trenches kept up their resistance in the first line, but at 7 o'clock they were finally driven out, and those who got across No Man's Land began to return to our trenches. After dark the battalion took up the position from which it started and remained there for the night and until the afternoon of the next day, when it was relieved and then withdrew to Bayencourt.*

Of the three assaulting companies, only 64 returned to the lines on the evening of 1 July; all of the officers were casualties.

Sergeant Sim was a casualty almost immediately he went over the top.

At 1 am our wire was cut, and at daylight when this was spotted the 'fun' began. The Germans shelled us heavily until our big bombardment commenced at 6.30 am. The shelling lasted for one hour and five minutes. Before it lifted on to the reserve trenches the smoke cloud was sent over and our boys began the advance. I was wounded on the left hand just as I had got on our parapet. Felt a bit dazed owing to a big crump having burst unpleasantly close just before. Didn't twig much that happened, but had sense enough to hop off quickly to the dressing station in Wurzel Street where Doctor Clarke bandaged the wound and told

JUNCTION
F FIR & FEN

JUNCTION
OF
EEL & FEAST

VILLAGE OF GOMMECOURT

WEST END OF EXE

GOMMECOURT. 1916.
Panorama taken on May 20th 1916,
from the Junction of W. 48 and W. 49 R.
See map page 127

> *me I should have to lose a finger. Walked to Sailly, got a private*
> *motor to clearing hospital at Couin and lorry from there to the*
> *railhead clearing hospital at Warlincourt.*

Captain Lindsey-Renton commanded the reserve company, D, and recorded his observations.

> *At 7.30 the attack commenced, the front line men advancing*
> *over the top just as though they were on parade, calmly and*
> *slowly while the reserve men stood on the parapet cheering them*
> *on. It was truly a weird sight as the troops gradually disappeared*
> *in the smoke. For some time nothing could be seen, but as the*
> *smoke began to clear away the advance could be followed. At*
> *one point the attacking party appeared to be held up and could*
> *be seen lining a bank, or the edge of a road* [this is the*
> Gommecourt-Puisieux road], *but after a time they got up and*
> *pushed forward.*

Sergeant Telfer, a platoon commander, explained what had happened at the road.

> *About twenty yards from our objective was a sunken road*
> *about six feet deep* [although sunken roads are still quite
> common on the Somme, in the 1914-1918 period they were all
> much deeper and considerably narrower. The process of
> widening them and metalling them has resulted in most of these
> sunken roads disappearing or being pale reflections of their
> former depth] *at which we were held up for some time, say ten*
> *minutes or a quarter of an hour, owing to the Boche fire being*
> *too heavy to climb up the bank and go forward. We were also*
> *subjected to heavy cross-fire on our right flank as the Rangers*
> *had not come up. It was here that poor Captain Cunningham was*
> *bowled over and I am of the opinion that he was killed, but of*
> *course one did not have the time to test his pulse - this is only my*
> *opinion and I hold very little hope for our poor skipper, for so*
> *many chaps were killed instantaneously with bullet wounds*
> *through the head when lying up on the bank pouring lead into*

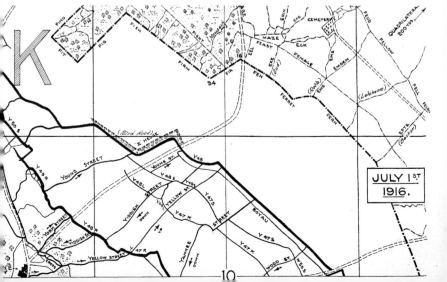

JUNCTION OF FERRET & FERN   JUNCTION OF FEMALE & FEED   GOMMECOURT CEMETERY   BRITISH FRONT LINE W. 50   JUNCTION FEUD & FELLOW

the Hun. [Captain Cunningham is commemorated on the Thiepval Memorial.]...*Quite on his own initiative, Lance Corporal Packer, the bombing corporal of No 1 Platoon, who led on our trek up the trenches, although wounded in the ear, rushed forward and bombed the Germans, followed instantaneously by several others, causing the occupants of the German third line to slacken their fire for a few seconds, and with the help of the QWR the third line was rushed and taken.*

Captain Lindsay-Renton continued his account, going on to describe the events of the afternoon.

During the afternoon it became clear that the situation at the front was bad and orders were received that at night the old German Front Line should be consolidated, but even that was found to be impossible. It was feared that the enemy, counting on the disorganisation resulting from the failure of the attack, would make a counter attack upon our original lines. Orders were accordingly issued to collect all available men, stragglers and anyone returning from the front, and occupy Y.47L, one of the assembly trenches, but not the first one, which was to be held at all costs. The counter-attack, however, never developed. About

Map 6. Attack area of the LRB and the QWR.

six o'clock a runner reached Battalion HQ after a very difficult and trying journey. This was Rfn Morris, quite a small youth. He arrived covered with mud and perspiration, delivered his message and then asked for some water. Having quenched his thirst he calmly sat down outside the HQ dugout and thoroughly cleaned his rifle! At dusk the survivors began to come in and a sad sight it was to see the remnant of the magnificent battalion that had gone forward that morning straggling back in twos and threes, tired to death, and completely overcome by the strain which they had been through.

Back in the transport lines was the second-in-command, Major Sampson. He went up to the trenches late in the evening and was horrified by what he saw.

We are filled with pride for all that has been done, bitterness for the little that there is to show for it, and sorrow for those we shall never see again. We are told we have, in fact, helped in the general scheme, and done our job, but the battalion is sadly mauled about. I feel that our job is done as regards actual fighting for many months and for, perhaps, the rest of the war [faint hope!]. Another feeling is unexpected: it is one of respect for the enemy. He fought well and finally showed himself not unchivalrous. Most of the wounded were, of course, in front of his trenches, and in the afternoon of the following day he waved handkerchiefs etc., and then his stretcher-bearers came out. Ours followed, and soon an informal armistice started. I, myself, and many others stood on top of our trenches and saw the stretcher bearers of both sides collecting and bringing in the

This photograph was taken two hundred yards to the south west of the 1916 panorama.

GOMMECOURT PARK   GOMMECOURT CEMETERY   GOMMECO

APPROXIMATE POSITION OF BRITISH FRONT LINE

JUNCTION OF FELL & FELON   ESSARTS   EPTE   NAMEL

wounded men.

The collection of the wounded went on for some time; the Germans made it clear that only unarmed men were to come over the parapet into No Man's Land - a few who had gone over with their rifles were shot at and some wounded. The truce was broken when the artillery started firing on the German right, and it was agreed that hostilities would recommence on the Gommecourt sector in ten minutes. Whatever the reason for the firing, it was to cost the lives of many wounded British soldiers and some of their German prisoners, who had become casualties making their way over to the British line.[6]

In fact Major Sampson was not to see much more of the war as he was invalided home a week later.

It is worth mentioning at this point that a soldier of the QVRs, Frank Hawkins, had his memoirs published in 1973, and although out of print, copies frequently appear on book lists from specialist book sellers. *From Ypres to Cambrai* covers his time with the regiment from his joining at the outbreak of war to his wounding at Gommecourt, and is an excellent read. He went on to a commission in the Royal Naval Division.

The Queen's Westminster Rifles (6/London Regiment) were to follow the QVRs from the assembly trenches and to pass over Fern and Feed; they were to be the centre part of the brigade's three battalion attack front. They were then to cross Fellow and capture Etch (a communication trench) and the Quadrilateral. They were then to secure the cross trenches to the east of the village, join up with the 46th Division in Fill and to consolidate Fillet, facing east, before proceeding to clear the village and park of Gommecourt. In effect the battalion was to follow the QVRs and use the third trench as a jumping off trench for the assault on the Quadrilateral. It was at this point that the

Queen's Westminster Rifles

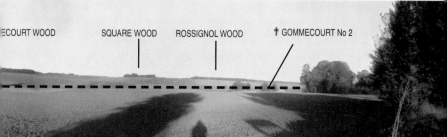

ECOURT WOOD   SQUARE WOOD   ROSSIGNOL WOOD   † GOMMECOURT No 2

Map 7. Gommecourt, 1 July 1916. The attack of the LRB.

Westminsters would have to go half left, as the alignment of the German trench system changed between their First and Second positions. It is worth pointing out here that trench systems were highly complex, and far more than just a ditch carved out of the earth. The Front Line would usually have a depth of two or three trenches, and this would be succeeded, at varying distances, according to strategic or tactical considerations, by a Second Line, in this case some 300-400 metres to the rear of the rear trench in the Front Line system.

The story of the advance was much as it was for the QVRs. A group of Westminsters made their way along Etch, gaining access where it crossed Nameless Road, that is the road between Gommecourt and Puisieux. They fought their way into Fellow, and then bombed their way along to the left, in the process of which they continued to lose heavily; however the momentum was continued, and a party progressed into Feud and towards the cemetery. There they met some stubborn resistance from a group of German bombers, but these were cleared in due course. At this point a battalion notice board was erected (of the type that Johnny Tucker prepared), and this encouraged men to join them from their position on the road.

Meanwhile another party, aided by men from 5/Cheshires, fought their way along Etch towards the east end of the Quadrilateral. They were driven back by the strong garrison and were forced to make a block at the junction of Etch and Fell. The blocks were constructed by this group, the Cheshires (men of the Pioneer battalion) and a party of RE whose job this, in part, was. A block, it should be mentioned in parenthesis, was just that - a trench had its walls blown or hacked down so that the enemy would be kept at a distance (preferably beyond bomb throwing distance) and could not work their way along the trench.

Meanwhile yet another party had attempted to reach the Quadrilateral via Ems, and succeeded in reaching it; here they continued the fight until they ran out of bombs. All of this had been achieved by about 9 am, and the QVR and the QWR were in possession of Fellow and Feud (that is the third German line) and the Cemetery. Attempts by D, the reserve company, to get a platoon forward, were met with a hail of shells and fire from the German Second Line, and got nowhere; the platoon was reduced to four survivors.

The Germans now started counter-attacking from the left, against the men of the London Rifle Brigade, whilst others started bombing down Ems; they decided to outflank the block by climbing out of Ems and gather to the north of the Cemetery; so that by 10.50 the enemy had pushed forward to this position, and indeed a full blooded battle was going on to the left of the battalion. A party from C Company managed to push the Germans back, all the way to the wood, and held them there for some ninety minutes. As time progressed the men were forced to the German front line, and a signal, by Venetian shutter, was observed by the RFC contact plane, with its plaintive message, 'SOS bombs'.

By 8.30 pm the last of the British troops who were able so to do had abandoned the German position; 198 men were the sad residue that went into billets at Bayencourt on 2 July. Reinforcements arrived, and were the circumstances not so tragic, the problems that they faced would seem comic. The battalion was put into the line in the Fonquevillers sector in the Z sector, to the rear of the Poplar. The trenches were in a terrible state; part of the fire trench was nearly three feet deep in water, and in the communications trenches the water was waist deep. Almost everyone took to taking their trousers off and tying their shirts between their legs. When the battalion went into the trenches on 6 July there went with them their draft of 268 men, many of whom were bantams - that is men who were below the standard height of five feet three inches. Thus they were particularly handicapped and indeed special arrangements had to be made, such as placing ammunition boxes on the parapet, so that they could carry out their duties.

London Rifle Brigade

To the left of the QWRs was the London Rifle Brigade (5/London Regiment). This regiment is doubly fortunate - it has an excellent regimental history[7] and it has a much more recent work, which examines the social as well as the military; what is more the author is interested in the battlefields themselves and thereby sees beyond the documents. This latter volume is still in print (1998, available, amongst other places, from the Imperial War Museum) and is most strongly recommended to those who would wish to pursue knowledge not only about what the LRB did in the Great War but also who they were.[8]

View from German Second Line near Rossignol Wood.

German Second Line · The Quad

The LRB was to assault with three strengthened companies (from right to left D, C and A) with B Company in reserve; the assaulting companies to go across in six waves. The regimental history records a series of personal statements made soon after the battle, and parts of these are here reproduced.

See map on page 56

Second Lieutenant RE Petley was a member of D Company. Before the battle he had been tasked with the laying of a tape a hundred and fifty yards ahead of the jumping off trenches; the first wave was to move forward to this line three minutes before zero to reduce the distance to cover in No Man's Land. The objectives for this company were Ferret, Exe, Female and Eck; Eck was to be consolidated with small posts whilst the position in general was strengthened. The first wave got straight to the objective, that is Eck, made contact with neighbouring troops and immediately got their wire up. They had trouble early on, though, from German snipers in the Park and the Cemetery and a machine gun from the rear.

At 8.30 am all seemed well; the commander of the forward Battalion HQ, Captain Somers-Smith, based at the junction of Exe and Fen, could be pleased with matters up to this point. But trouble was brewing, as Petley records.

> Then a QVR man came and reported that he had lost touch with his regiment and that only about a dozen of his men were on our right, also, that they were being bombed. Smith (an officer in D) went along to see what he could do and a message was sent back to HQ in Exe. I believe a party of battalion bombers tried to cut them off in the rear. However it soon became evident to us that the Huns were bombing uncomfortably near us on the right, and Captain de Cologan moved further down Eck towards Exe. I found myself in a sort of cul-de-sac and managed to get into the main trench (if it can be so called) by making each man crawl singly over a big mound of earth, while we kept the Huns on our right down with bombs and sniping. As soon as we were all over, we turned the mound into a barricade and managed easily enough to hold the Germans back.

Here he became isolated from the rest of the battalion, and could not get a message through. Eventually, with bombs fast running out, he sent a somewhat pointed message at 4pm.

> I sent a message to you about two hours ago to the effect that I am holding on to Eck with about forty men, including a dozen QVR and one QWR and that I wanted more bombs. Quite out of touch to right and left. Have held off Germans on our right with

This photograph of Gommecourt Church was taken about a month after its capture in 1917.

barricade. It is quite absurd to lay here at night as we are.
Eventually a message got through to him to abandon the position; reluctantly he decided to leave the wounded behind as the Germans launched a considerable bombing attack from female; the party made their way southwards via Maze and into Fibre, just beyond Feast. The move was hazardous.

We had no less than four different bombing parties to keep off, and the whole of my party got to the German second trench with only two or three casualties. It was in the independent rushes across the open, of course, that the casualties occurred, but even then, most of us, I believe, got to the German front trench. Austin and I lay in a shell hole by the second line to cover as much as possible these final rushes. Our intention was to stay there until dark, but on a bomb bursting in our shell hole we cleared off before the smoke lifted. Austin muttered that he was hit, but we did not wait to argue. We ran in different directions and I have not seen him. Although the bomb practically burst on us, I was unhurt except for a few tiny pieces in my legs.

When the time came to abandon the German lines at about 8.30 pm, he was wounded in the rush to get across (this time in the knee); *'you can imagine the waiting till dark and crawling in etc.'*

> *There is an incident I should like to mention which shows that we had a decent lot of Huns opposite, and which would prove a source of consolation to the relatives of the missing. About 9.45 pm (early twilight) a German came out to us, and as I saw his red cross I prevented our men from firing. He came up, saw I had been roughly dressed, and went on nearer to our own lines to attend to one of his own men. Some of our men got up to go, and he shouted out and stopped one of their machine guns. I think his action showed pluck and decency, and augurs well for the wounded whom we had to leave behind.*

Lance Corporal Foaden in C Company (the centre attacking company) gave his account of the action; he was in the fifth wave which encountered heavy machine gun and artillery fire straight away, especially after coming out of the smoke about fifty yards after they set off.

> *The enemy was found in his dugouts in Feast. I saw two taken prisoner and others shot or bombed. On reaching the Maze, which was little more than large shell holes, I bore to the left and took shelter in a large shell hole. ... There were about ten men at this point, which we held and commenced to consolidate at once. Snipers were very busy and killed one and wounded two during the first two minutes. We were filling sandbags whilst lying down, until there was sufficient cover to work our Lewis gun. We*

This is an example of the conditions endured in the trenches after heavy rainfall turned them into quagmires.

View from Gommecourt Cemetery, where there was so much heavy fighting, towards Gommecourt Park and Gommecourt.

> proceeded to consolidate the position as far as possible until 12.45 pm, when we realised the futility of working further, owing to the continual landslides.

About 4 pm they were ordered back by Sergeant Hember, but Foaden said that this would be impracticable until the cover of dusk. Soon after this enemy bombers appeared in Fibre.

> I opened fire with the Lewis gun, whereupon the enemy threw up his hands, I took this to be a ruse and fired again. This occurred on three occasions. I then retired towards the Maze, taking the gun with me. I saw the enemy again there and once more fired. I was now covering a large shell hole in which were Sergeant Hember and fourteen men. Having but two grenades, we decided to try and reach the rest of the battalion, so I stripped the gun, rendering it useless to the enemy. The premature explosion of one of our own grenades wounded Sergeant Hember and five others. I then decided to retire with the remainder and get reinforcements. After several fruitless attempts to find Fen we managed to work round the outer edge of Maze and reached Exe. On reaching Female we found more German bombers, at whom we fired and threw our last grenade. We had just previously passed four enemy dugouts, in one of which was Rfn WG Bates wounded and a prisoner. Near by were two wounded Germans. We eventually crawled down Exe and reached the remainder of the battalion. The enemy was kept at bay until the last grenade had been thrown. Bombing had been kept up for some time by means of grenades captured from the enemy.

Lewis gunner gets into position.

For his work on this day, Foaden was awarded the Military Medal. Sergeants Lilley and Frost provided accounts of what happened to A Company. Lilley reported that,

> The first wave found the wire in

front of point 94 well cut by our artillery, but the wire used was very thick and owing to it being in long lengths was still an obstacle and had to be cut and trampled down. By the time this was completed the second wave advanced from our trenches and came up to us without any trouble. It got through the German front line easily. On reaching there, Second Lieutenant Doust was shot through the head by a German officer, whom we killed.

(Doust is commemorated on the Thiepval Memorial. He joined the regiment on 6 August 1914 and had already been badly wounded during the Second Battle of Ypres.)

The men cleared the trench from Firm through Fir and Eel to Feast, but faced constant pressure from bombers who were covered by snipers. The left flank was guarded by the establishment of a Lewis gun position at the junction of Fen and Fir, which then traversed the left front to keep the enemy back. The position was held until about 7.45pm.

No equipment of any kind was worn by any Germans seen all day, grenades being carried in sandbags. We found the front line full of deep dugouts supplied with bunks for sleeping in. there was a plentiful supply of food on the shelves. We had to leave behind us in a dugout all the casualties which had taken place in the enemy lines who could not make their own way back. We also left a party of 16 prisoners in the next dugout.

A view of the remains of Gommecourt during a lull in the 1916 offensive.

Lilley was rather reticent in his account about his own achievements, described by Sergeant Frost, and for which he got the DCM, gazetted in September 1916.

> *We managed to hold on to our bit of trench, however, and, in fact, it was the last piece of enemy trench to be evacuated. The credit for this is certainly due to Sergeant Lilley, who worked very hard and courageously throughout the day. I cannot say how much I admired his behaviour. Another who helped greatly was a youngster* [Rfn Reynolds] *working the Lewis gun posted in our trench* [around point 94]. *He kept so cool and never hesitated to expose himself.*

There were many acts of individual heroism during the day. The CO of the QVRs sent a memo to his opposite number in the LRB after the battle about the courage of Rfn Hudson, accompanying a report by one of his officers, and noting himself that he concurred, adding,

> *Rfn Coventry of my battalion also gave me the same report at the time of delivering the message at my headquarters on Z day, saying what a brave fellow Rfn Hudson of your battalion was; his only thought was his duty, although badly wounded. I hope the poor fellow is alright.*

The original report, by Second Lieutenant Ord-Mackenzie of the QVRs (who himself was killed in later fighting on the Somme on 24 September, and has no known grave), was unstinting in his praise.

> *I have the honour to bring to your notice the gallant conduct of No 647 Rfn CH Hudson of the LRB on the morning of July 1st in conveying and delivering messages from the advanced companies whilst severely wounded. The circumstances were as follows: at some time between 11 am and noon I was in Y47 between Yankee Street and Yellow Street together with Rfn Coventry examining the ground with a view to crossing to the German lines. I had stopped to adjust the bandage of a wounded man, when Rfn Hudson came into the trench from the direction of the enemy's lines and collapsed, shouting that he had two messages and asking me to take the delivery of them. I read the messages and endorsed them and, upon examining his wound found him badly wounded in the stomach. I bandaged him to the best of my ability with a field dressing, whereupon he expressed himself able to reach headquarters if helped. As the messages contained the answer to one carried by Rfn Coventry I decided to send him back to assist Rfn Hudson, and to deliver his message. Rfn Coventry asserts that Rfn Hudson displayed great*

courage and fortitude throughout, and I should like to call attention to the fact that his first thought, when he met me, was for his duty and not for himself. He stated that he was the third to make the attempt. I propose to allow Rfn Coventry to read this report and affix his signature to signify that he is in agreement with the details thereof.

Colonel Dickins also added his signature; all of which suggests that it was hoped that the action of Hudson would result in a high award, possibly the VC. However he died of his wounds in a hospital on the coast, and is buried at Le Treport; and the VC was the only medal that could be awarded posthumously, which he failed to get. Rfn Coventry went on to win the Military Medal in the December of 1916, and survived the war.

Three out of four men who were killed in the LRB have no known grave and are commemorated at Thiepval.

Joseph McGrath

Amongst these is Joseph McGrath, a twenty four year old member of C Company, typical of the sort of man who joined these London territorial battalions. He was a promising soldier who, again quite typically, declined - along with a number of his friends - to go on for a commission. He was a pupil of my own school, and in the archives there are a number of papers relating to his life and death. His obituary is of a sort that is repeated in numerous school magazines all over the country. It is worth bearing in mind that in those days of boarding education at the turn of the century, holidays, apart from the very long summer break, were short, in fact almost non-existent. Therefore a strong attachment (or loathing!) grew between pupil and school, especially if they were educated there for several years. McGrath was no exception. He was no great brain but he did well at both work and games. He was captain of the school in his last terms.

Everywhere he went - in England, Ireland, America, France and Italy - he found and kept his friends; and I feel sure that to all who knew him, he was to the end of his life the boy in the best, the manly sense of the word. Simply, he did not know how to grow up and be spoiled by the world, and the keynote of his life was joy. He had that rare cleverness of extracting the best from everyone and everything, and therefore he enjoyed life. From Birmingham he wrote that though he did not relish New Street, 'he had met with such jolly people'. In America he found everyone, 'just splendid'; in Paris 'the people were awfully kind'; in Italy, 'they just did all they could for him'.

Quotes from his letters are given:

April 17 1916 The birds don't seem to mind the firing

June 12 1916 The country around this neighbourhood is really very pretty, and everything that meets the eye is a very beautiful green. The most annoying part of all is, however, that it seems as though the rain will never leave us.

McGrath had left Ratcliffe College in 1909 and went into business in London. In due course he gained further experience in America before returning to Europe, and some time after his return he took up a good position in Genoa, which he relinquished, without hesitation, when the war started. He returned with three friends, and joined the LRB. Before going over the top he wrote a letter, as was common, to his parents. He left it with his other surplus equipment in his billet with the following written on the envelope:

In the event of me being killed, please post enclosed letter. If wounded only, anyone finding this letter will kindly tear it up.

The letter, dated 27 June 1916, reads:

I have just written you a few lines, but this letter will not be posted to you to-day. I sincerely hope it may not have to be sent to you at all.

For some time past our Regiment has known that it would be its duty, sooner or later, to go over the top and take some German trenches.

Well, the moment has at last come, and everybody hopes the London Rifle Brigade is going to add to its list of honours and make a great name for itself. It may be tomorrow, or the day after, when the task will be set us, and, as is only natural, there will be casualties, probably very heavy judging by the nature of the work.

I am writing these few lines in case I may be one of the unfortunate - or rather unlucky - ones who will have to go under, as there is sure to be a heavy percentage of killed.

Need I say all the fellows are in the best of spirits and eager to get face to face with the Germans, and there is not one who would shirk going into the charge - at least it can hardly be called that!

Don't worry at all, dearest father ad mother, should anything serious happen to me. I have not the least fear of death, and, all through, this life has been more like a huge sport to me. Hundreds of thousands of other fellows have died willingly for the same cause, and certainly thousands more will have to die yet before this war will come to an end.

On Sunday last I was very fortunate in being near a Church and was able to go to Confession and Communion, so I have not much to worry about.

You cannot realise, dearest father and mother, what your parcels have meant to me and how much pleasure I really obtained from them.

The order has just come through at this moment, unexpectedly, for us to march off at once.

Heaps and heaps of love to yourselves and all,

Ever your loving son, Joe.

His father died soon afterwards, grief-stricken at the loss of his only son and of a favourite nephew, who was killed a few months earlier.

The battalion was bitter with what happened after the battle, typical of the complaints of many of the London Territorial battalions.

Great determination, combined with good discipline, is necessarily required if the daily routine of a regiment is to be carried on after a long preparation and a heavy engagement, just

*when the inevitable reaction is being felt and the extent and
nature of its losses realised. It was a great blow, and one that was
much felt at this trying time, for the regiment to receive a large
draft, not from its own 3rd Battalion (the reserve battalion, based
in the UK), but from 2/7 Middlesex, which had been serving for
eighteen months in Egypt... There was at this time a large draft
of the LRB actually in France at the base, which made the matter
all the worse, and it was no consolation to know that all the
regiments were treated alike, or that the QVR had
representatives of no less than seventeen different units in its
ranks. It is difficult to write temperately about the course of
action pursued by those in authority...*

It is an important point to note that the compilers of the regimental
history wax lyrical about this issue, but make hardly any adverse
comments about either the planning, or the conduct or the reason
(when it was made apparent) for the attack on Gommecourt on 1 July.
It is a graphic illustration of how vital in the mind of many - perhaps
most - was the 'family' that was the battalion.

The reserve battalion of the brigade was 2/London Regiment (City
of London) and it too suffered heavy casualties, though not to the same
extent as its fellow brigade members. Brigadier Coke, commanding
169 Brigade (which job he retained until the end of the war) decided in
the early afternoon, at about 1.30 pm, that the situation had to be
retrieved by committing his reserve, throwing back the German
incursions from the left and bringing up urgently required bombs. The
reserve company moved up to a position to the right of Z Hedge whilst
the other companies prepared to attack: A against Fern and Fever, with
the objective of Female; D against Ferret and C against Fir and Fen
with the objective of Feast in the second line. The attack was to be
launched just after 2.30 pm.

C set off from the right end of Z Hedge, and formed up outside the
wire. They were swept in enfilade by machine gun fire from the Park
and soon lost all their officers, so that only a few actually made it to
the German line, let alone do what was required. A Company melted
away as it crossed No Man's Land - of five officers and 90 other ranks
who had left the trench, only ten returned unwounded. D Company was
late in assembly, and thus did not arrive before C was already being
mercilessly swept away; they were saved by the delay, because the
Brigadier ordered their attack to be halted (on representations from
their battalion commander, who could see all that was going on from
his advanced headquarters). The battalion was then ordered to prepare

to move forward and take over the German line at dusk; but events put that idea to rest and instead they consolidated the British line. The remnants of C and A companies totalled about fifty; hardly any of these were unwounded.[10]

In various parts of the narrative in these regimental histories there are references to 5/Cheshires which was serving at the Pioneer Battalion for the division. The regimental history's entry for this battalion is laconic in the extreme:

> On the whole front of attack (ie the front of 1 July) only one Cheshire company went over with the first wave at zero, 7.30 am on July 1st. This was A Company of the 5th Battalion. The company was split up among the attacking battalions of 169 Brigade, with the task of constructing strongpoints (to facilitate the holding of the new German line).
>
> This attack had a wide No Man's Land to cross, no less than 800 yards. It would have been double this but for a fine piece of work by the battalion some weeks earlier in making a new jumping-off trench.
>
> A Company lost all its officers and 130 men.
>
> C Company had a similar task with 168 Brigade, but orders miscarried and the company remained inactive.
>
> B Company had the task of removing barricades and making trench bridges [so that the troops did not have to clamber in and out of trenches] as the attack progressed, and carried out all its tasks.
>
> 3 officers and 43 men were killed; 5 officers and 154 NCOs and men were wounded.

A rather more worthy account is provided by *Subalterns of the Foot*, the experiences of a number of officers who started their overseas service in 5/Cheshires, none of whom actually was present at Gommecourt as two had left the battalion and one was seriously ill with fever. Nevertheless there is an excellent account of what happened at Gommecourt on 1 July to the battalion, as well as insights in its life before and after that fateful day. The book (in 1998) is still available.[11]

The battle was over - just about fourteen hours between the time that the first British soldiers had piled over the top and out of their assembly positions to the abandoning of the German line in which so much confused and bitter fighting had taken place. It was truly a disastrous day for the 56th Division, but one from which it recovered, licked its wounds, rebuilt and was much wiser. It was the story of a large part of the British Army. One of the ironies in this particular story is that the casualties of the division were so high because it had had a measure of success and had held on for so long; the 46th Division's battle was over within, realistically, minutes - and although its losses were very severe, they were almost 2,000 less than those of the 56th. The London Rifle Brigade and the London Scottish had the dubious distinctions of having the highest casualties in the division.

1. Most of the information in this section of the chapter comes from *The London Scottish in the Great War,* ed Lieutenant Colonel JH Lindsay DSO. Regimental Headquarters,1926.

2. *The 'Kensingtons' 13th London Regiment,* Sergeant OF Bailey and Sergeant HM Hollier. Regimental Old Comrades Association n.d.

3. The introduction by John Masefield to *Attack on the Somme,* Edward G Living 1918. It has been reprinted by Spa Books (1986) and is still available. This quote taken from the Rangers history, *op cit.*

4. *Attack on the Somme, op cit.*

5. *The Rangers' Historical Records from 1859 to the conclusion of the Great War* ed Captain AV Wheeler-Holohan and Captain GMG Wyatt. Chenies Street n.d.

6. *The History and Records of Queen Victoria's Rifles 1792-1922* compiled Major CA Cuthbert Keeson VD. Constable and Co Ltd 1923.

7. *The History of the London Rifle Brigade anon.* Constable and Co Ltd 1921

8. *Gentlemen and Officers The Impact and Experience of War on a Territorial Regiment 1914 - 1918* KW Mitchinson. The Imperial War Museum 1995.

9. Mitchinson, *op cit.*

 Provincial Archives of the Institute of Charity (Ratcliffe): The Great War

10. *The 2nd City of London Regiment (Royal Fusiliers) in the Great War (1014 - 19)* Major WE Grey. Regimental Headquarters 1929.

11. *Subalterns of the Foot: Three World War I diaries of officers of the Cheshire Regiment* Anne Wolff. Square One Publications 1992.

Chapter Three

THE 46TH DIVISION BEFORE THE BATTLE

The 46th Division, unlike the 56th, had been in France for a long time (sixteen months) by the time that 1 July came along - it arrived in Le Havre at the end of February 1915. In fact it was the first complete Territorial division to arrive in France, indeed the first to arrive in any war theatre. It had had some quite difficult times, notably extemely heavy casualties in October 1915 on the Loos battlefield, around Hohenzollern Redoubt and had had an uncomfortable time on Vimy Ridge when the British first took over the line there in February 1916. The trenches were very poor; whilst they were there Germans launched what was described by a Brigade Major as, 'the best executed large trench raid of the war' and they faced a daily threat of being blown up by one of the numerous German mines burrowed under their lines. For more details of this latter period, see my *Vimy Ridge* in this series. At the beginning of May the division made its way southwards. The 1/5th Leicesters found themselves billeted in Lucheux, a small village a few kilometres to the north east of Doullens which owed its existence to an ancient castle, then a ruin, and a chateau, which became brigade headquarters. Nearby was a forest and many men in the brigade (138) were put to work in the nearby, and vast, Lucheux wood, making wattle fencing to be used as revetments (supports for the trenches).

In fact the historian of the 1/4th Leicesters devoted a small chapter to the pleasures of this particular part of the battalion's history.

The battalion was very happy. There were wars and rumours of offensives. But it mattered little because the men had got it into their heads that they were out for a good rest and that they thoroughly deserved it...The trenches at Vimy had been notoriously bad; anywhere in the line they were likely to be sent would be more salubrious; it could not be worse.

He goes on,

And so the 4th Leicesters became clean, smart, well-drilled, full of esprit de corps, and everything that a good battalion ought to be. There were route marches. There was training of all sorts. Bombers bombed. Machine gunners looked busy under a tree in the corner of the field. Scouts crawled about on their bellies, peered industriously through field glasses to see if there were any brass hats or skirts in sight, and then studied the idiosyncrasies of the compass until tea-time. And as for the snipers, they spent so many hours of daylight turning the bottom of a dry ditch into a really comfortable sniper's post that it seemed a pity not to take the better looking of the farmer's daughters to inspect it by moonlight.

The battalion was inspected by the brigadier - it had regimental sports. Many historians complain about the value of regimental histories, arguing that they often do not contribute much to the military story of the war, and they are dismissive of such things as pages spent on sports and regimental horse shows. But this seems to me to miss the point and purpose of these histories, which were a chronicle of what happened to a regiment, or often a battalion. To these men, these sports days were memorable - more so, because they were a rarity in a life of drudgery in the trenches, periodic extreme trauma during a battle or patrol and only rarely was there the luxury of regular hours, food and assured relaxation. Thus both the 5th and 4th Leicesters historians spend some time on the needle soccer match between them, won by 4/Leicesters 3-2.

The period spent at work in Lucheux wood proved to be a most happy time.

It was a nine days' wonder. It was a wonderful nine days. 9 am to 4.30 pm. Generally 200 men. Sometimes 500 men. It was a delightful way of spending the merry month of May. The wood was shady. The birds sang in the trees. The bill-hooks whistled through the wattles. Contented soldiers whistled through their teeth. Wattle revetments were mass-produced in the happiest factory in the world.

But the war called; in mid May they moved on and *'left the Forset of Lucheux a worse place than they had found it'.* 4/Leicesters moved into huts in Humbercamps, the history adding its own ominous comment, *'the nearer the line the colder the feet'.*

Of course this was not entirely a rural interlude; training was very much a part of the process, not without its casualties. For example,

Second Lieutenant JA Cooper, the battalion bombing officer of 1/7th Sherwood Foresters (Notts and Derby), was killed on 17 May in an accident whilst instructing his men; he is buried in Humbercamps Communal Cemetery Extension. 4/Leicesters had the pleasure of hearing a two hour lecture from the notorious Major Campbell of the Army Gymnastic Staff on the subject of the use of the bayonet.

He held the attention of a hall full of all ranks, speaking so vividly that not one of us but came away feeling that we were good enough to fight six Boche, given

Outside Battalion HQ at Fonquevillers, June 1916, Lt. Col. J H Thursfield, M.C.

a bayonet. He was particularly insistent on not driving the bayonet home too far, and we shall always remember his 'throat two inches is enough, kidney only four inches, just in and out'.

Campbell must have been very good at his job, because his lectures certainly seemed to have fixed themselves in the memory of innumerable men who wrote their memoirs after the war, whether they were revolted or enthused by his antics.

Whilst the Leicesters had been having a relatively leisurely time, the Staffordshire Brigade (137) had moved from the Vimy sector into Fonquevillers itself. The village was only about four hundred yards or so from the front line, but was not badly knocked about (indeed one farmer was still ploughing away within a thousand yards of the line) and many houses (and more particularly their cellars) were intact. The history of 5/North Staffords put this down to the local topography.

Thanks to the contour of the country, and the large number of trees, troops could walk about the village with considerable impunity, although it was not comfortable to loiter near the church and cross roads. The road leading to Souastre was open to wheeled traffic and even troops in broad daylight. The enemy did not shell the trenches to any great extent, but indulged in a certain amount of practice with a heavy mortar by night. There

Any damaged building which could be made more weather proof was put to use in the rear of the firing-trenches. The photograph shows a dilapidated village building with its thatched roof still remaining moderately intact; it is occupied by an officer of rank as indicated by the presence of a sentry near the main entrance.

were a considerable number of communications trenches leading from the village to the front line, but the majority of these had not been kept up during the winter, and if not impassable, were in a very bad state of repair. The front line had been held by posts during the winter, and the trenches between the posts were filled in by wire, so that a visit from one post to another necessitated a considerable detour. The work of improving the trenches and of removing the wire, commenced almost immediately, and rumours of an impending attack were soon started.

This task on the trenches was shared with their sister battalion, 6/South Staffords. They replaced the Leicesters at Lucheux, in due course, with the added task of digging the practice trenches. This was not at all popular with the local French farmers, and despite the fact that they received compensation some of them took to referring to the British as 'les autres boches'. Elsewhere the work needed to make what had been a quiet sector into one fit to support a battle took its toll of the battalions. Cable trenches were dug from headquarters in the rear to forward batteries and observation posts, building and stocking ammunition and bomb stores, and assisting in the construction of numerous gun pits.

The work was very hard, for digging a narrow trench, or loading flints at Warlincourt quarries (to the north of Pas) are no light tasks, and the weather made conditions even more difficult than they might otherwise have been. One day it was so hot as to make continuous work for more than a few hours impossible, while the next, there would be three or four torrential rain storms, filling all the trenches, and turning the cross country tracks into avenues of mud.

Rehearsals were carried out meticulously; the Robin Hoods (7/Sherwood Foresters) reported that the practice trenches must have been attacked fifty times. Men were taught their tasks down to the individual and practised with live bombs and smoke screens. But the unpredictable weather was beginning to prove to be a serious problem.

The weather had completely changed the condition of the trenches; in the communications trenches and the fire [front] trenches it was difficult to find a place where the muddy water came below the knees, and for long stretches it was up to the thighs. The effects of this disastrous weather were far-reaching; they were, in fact, a deciding factor in the attack. Large sections of trenches collapsed altogether, their sides simply sliding in, being undermined by the water. Bomb shelters, ammunition

Map 8. Extract from Trench map: Fonquevillers 57D NE Sheet 1&2 dated 27.12.16.

dumps, ration stores etc. fared likewise. Add to this the damage done by hostile shelling, and the necessary drainage of the trenches to make them even passable with difficulty and the reader will understand something of the problem confronting the staff, as to how to get the sector ready for the attack, when only ten days remained.

The history accepted that the work had to be done, but could not see why it had to be the attacking battalion doing it; but, in truth, the expression 'all hands to the pump' is the most apposite description of how the men of the division found themselves engaged in these torrid conditions, with all the manpower becoming exhausted with this vital preparatory work. For example 5/North Staffords made similar complaints.

The weather, on the whole, was bad, and the local accommodation totally insufficient for housing the troops employed, who consequently had to content themselves with such rough shelter as could be provided. All this labour, too, had to be carried out in addition to the fighting, and to the everyday work of maintaining existing defences. It threw a very heavy strain on the troops, which was borne by them with a cheerfulness beyond all praise.

This work was made even more wearying by the need to return to billets afterwards, a round trip of eighteen miles, for example, for 5/North Staffords.

Rather late in the day, it was decided that the distance across No Man's Land had to be shortened and so it was determined to dig a jumping off trench forward of the British line. The attack was to be launched from the left of the Fonquevillers-Gommecourt road; the most notable feature of the right flank was the remains of the Sucrerie, the site of which is about twenty yards or so on the opposite side of the road from Gommecourt Wood British cemetery. In fact on this flank the lines were quite close, and the jumping off trenches were chiefly required for the left hand side of the attack, in front of the German position known as the Little Z.

This work was to be done by 6/South and 6/North Staffords, with 5/North and 5/South Staffords providing covering parties for the workmen.

The new line had to be taped out by the engineers, and detailed preparations made for the new trench and also communication trenches leading to it. These were to be completed in one night. As soon as darkness permitted, the covering parties took up their position, and were followed immediately by the working parties of the two battalions. Silence was essential, since the slightest sound of digging would have given the position away and, owing to the close proximity of the enemy, make the task impossible.

All went well on the first night, and a trench some four to five feet deep, complete with communication trenches to the British line, had been constructed. But this was not sufficient, and the work had to be completed the following night. In fact the enemy had fired a shell during the day to register (ie set an accurate range) the new line, which indicated that things would not be so easy on the following night.

Unlike the previous night, the conditions when work resumed were most unfavourable. Heavy rain

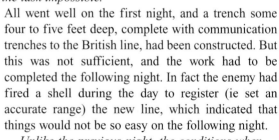

Brigadier-General C T Shipley CB. Commanding Sherwood Foresters' Brigade.

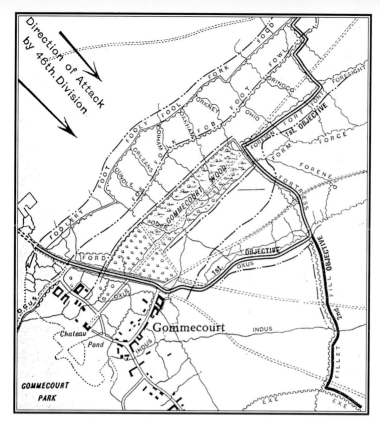

Map 9. The 46th Division attack on Gommecourt, July 1 1916.

*had fallen which made the trenches almost waist deep in water.
No useful work could be done, and no pumps were available for
clearing the water. Our troops must have been heard by the
enemy as they made their way to the new trench, and the best
they could do when they got there was to bale the water out with
their steel helmet. Rain was pouring in torrents, and from the
exposed position in the front line it was difficult to keep
telephone communications with the artillery. The situation
remained quiet until 12.20 am when, without preliminary
warning, the enemy guns opened, and for a quarter of an hour or
so a heavy fire was directed on our working parties. Those who
were not prevented by the depth of water managed to take cover
in the new trench; others who were caught in the open suffered
heavily. The fire ceased as quickly as it had begun, and the
casualties were brought in.*

Battalions due to take part in the assault had suffered heavy loss; but
perhaps more significant was the strength and accuracy shown by the

German artillery. Indeed, work parties behind the line got hit as well; thus 5/North Staffs also had men working on trenches just behind the old British line, and an officer recorded his memories of the night.

It was fearfully muddy and wet. Captain Wenger went into one hole almost up to his chest. I took my party off to the left, spread them out and set them digging. The trench was about two feet deep, one foot of it consisting of liquid mud [this trench would be used as an assembly trench for the attack]. *We were about fifty yards behind the front line. The 6th North were digging a trench for the attack 150 yards in front of the old line and 100 yards from the Hun. We could hear the clink of pick and shovel, and they were talking. The Hun was very quiet; except for a few flares he did nothing. Too little, in fact, for one felt mischief brewing. I was walking up and down by the trench, but met Captain Wenger, who advised me to find 'a hole', and keep my eye on it - in case.*

For half or three quarters of an hour things went on quietly. Quite suddenly, about 12.30 (am), heavy machine gun fire broke out to our front. I located my hole but did not get in. It suddenly increased in volume and I dived in. At the same time heavy shelling and mortar fire was directed at us. I was sharing my cranny with my sergeant, and we lay very flat in the mud. Bullets flirted through the scanty parapet which had been thrown up and pieces of shell metal whizzed down and hit the ground near us, and I contrived to make my tin hat a kind of umbrella but, peering under the edge, the air seemed to be full of dazzling flashes and puffs of smoke - just visible against the sky. The only comment one made was, 'Where the blazes are our artillery?' The firing gradually stopped, after about six minutes, and the message was passed down, 'Anyone hurt?' Luckily none of my party had suffered. We sat tight a while, and then came the order, 'File out.' We started to do so, but a sharp burst of shelling checked us! It was then our own guns replied, the whole sky behind us was instantaneously lit up with a great white light, and

1/6 North Staffs crossing Burton Bridge, August 1914.

almost at once our own shells rushed overhead.

The main communication trench was a weird experience. We got scattered in it, but I pushed down to Church Corner, where I got most of my lot together. The trench itself was packed with men, scrambling and sliding in the mud, but making way for 'walking wounded' and 'stretchers'.

This little escapade cost the Stafford Brigade almost 100 casualties.

As well as this reversal of fortune, various patrols sent out during the seven day bombardment to investigate the German lines and capture German prisoners all failed dismally. That by 4/Leicesters was decided by their own side - in this case the artillery.

Suddenly there is a burst of red hot hail. Suddenly optimistic British soldiers crawling on their bellies give a cough and a grunt and lie still. Others shriek with pain. The surprise party is surprised. And doubly surprised, because the salvo of shrapnel comes not from the Hun batteries behind Gommecourt, but from the British front. The men are bewildered...To get the wounded away in safety is now the problem. The fragments that remain are gathered up, and .. the party haltingly retire bearing their dead and wounded with them. ..A wounded man is carried on a ladder back to the British line, only to find on arrival that all his brains are shot away... A certain battery commander gets straffed.

Thus does the battalion history sardonically describe this disastrous patrol.

The final bird of ill-omen was the decision to postpone the attack for forty eight hours because of the weather. It was decided that the attacking brigades could not possibly stay in the appalling conditions of the assembly trenches for this time, and so they were withdrawn - but to busy themselves in doing further rehearsals back at Lucheux (eleven miles away) and then to march back again for the rescheduled attack. The two brigades, 137 and 139, were very tired by the time that the signal for the attack came through.[1]

1. The sources for this and the next chapter come from the following:
'The Robin Hoods' 1/7th, 2/7th and 3/7th Battalions Sherwood Foresters 1914 - 1918. Written by officers of the Battalions. J & H Bell Ltd. 1921
Footprints of the 1/4th Leicestershire Regiment August 1914 to November 1918 John Milne. Edgar Backus 1935
The Fifth Leicestershire, Captain JD Hills MC. Loughborough 1919
The Fifth North Staffords and the North Midland Territorials (The 46th and 59th Divisions) 1914 - 1919. Lieutenant W Meakin. Hughes & Barber Ltd., 1920
The War History of the Sixth Battalion the South Staffordshire Regiment (TF), a Committee of Officers who served with the Battalion. William Heinemann Ltd, 1924
The History of the Lincolnshire Regiment 1914 - 1918, ed Major-General CR Simpson CB. The Medici Society Ltd., 1931

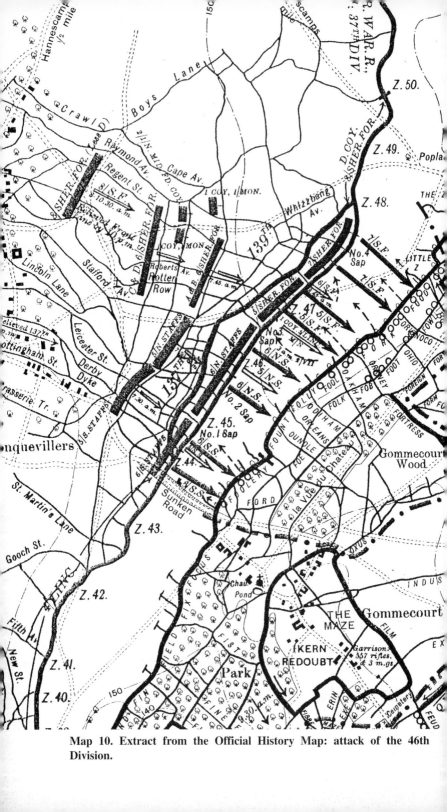

Map 10. Extract from the Official History Map: attack of the 46th Division.

Chapter Four

THE ATTACK OF THE 46TH DIVISION - AND THE AFTERMATH

The account of the battle at Gommecourt in 4/Leicesters history has got to be one of the most laconic of any battle in any regimental history.

> *The Staffords relieve the battalion on June 30th. Gommecourt is attacked on July 1st. The attack fails. The 4th Leicesters are reserve battalion of the reserve brigade. They are not sent to the slaughter. The Staffords and Sherwoods lose heavily.*
>
> *The taps of the Somme blood bath are full on.*

Robin Hoods 1/7 Sherwood Foresters

The dubious honour of being the northernmost battalion engaged in the attack on 1 July fell to 7/Sherwood Foresters. They would attack from just south west of the Little Z. The men moved up from their billets in Bienvillers to Fonquevillers in the course of the afternoon of 30 June and there collected all the relevant trench stores (barbed wire, picks, shovels, sandbags, trench ladders etc) and then rested, enjoying a last meal of huge bacon sandwiches. At 9 pm they started their move up to the front, a move which was made extremely arduous because of the flooded communication trenches (in this case Raymond Avenue, Regent Street and Roberts Avenue) and heavy loads. This was especially true of D Company, whose task it was to carry over most of

Germans in a wood at Gommecourt, July 1916.

these trench stores after the other companies had secured their position in the German lines. Because of the frequent stoppages as the men moved forward; and because they dared not put down their loads in case they got lost in the mud; and because the trenches were so waterlogged, these men in particular had a horrendous journey, often having to be heaved out of the mud into which they had sunk above their knees. They were shattered by the time they got to their assembly position. Things were not much better there, most of the men unable to find any means of relaxing because of the depth of the water in the trenches, and having to make do with leaning against the walls.

The photograph shows the conditions of the trenches after continuous heavy rainfall. This is a flooded communication trench.

Matters were made worse by the fact that the crowded trenches precluded the removal of any casualties, a situation that only worsened when the Germans started shelling the assembly lines at dawn.

The attack was to be launched in five waves, A, B and C in the first waves with D, the carrying company, in the fifth. Matters went awry almost immediately with the smoke discharge, fired off a few minutes before zero, which proved to be too thick and which resulted (as had happened to elements in the 56th Division) in loss of direction and cohesion. The first wave set off from the new jumping off trench, and the second wave followed from the front line. The enemy fire hit the third and fourth waves particularly hard, almost eliminating them. The carrying party had to move forward through the communications trenches and only managed to set off across No Man's Land at 8 am

By this stage the smoke had largely cleared - so the men were fighting their way through smoke, with all the dislocation that that caused, for the first seventy or so yards from the British line, and then emerged into full vision between there and the German line.

The first waves managed to get the grand total of a dozen or so men into the second line; they fell back and made the front line with five remaining. There they joined with twenty or so men who had organised themselves into a fire position of sorts. The Germans rapidly ejected them with bombing attacks from either flank, whilst the defenders themselves soon ran out of bombs and most found their rifles useless because of the mud and water. Those that were left took refuge in shell holes in No Man's Land. Some bombers had made it almost to the German third line, but since they were completely unsupported, they had no option but to join others in No Man's Land.

Another early casualty had been the CO, Lieutenant Colonel Hind. He and his adjutant accompanied the first wave over and then took shelter in a shell hole about fifty yards from the German line. He raised himself up on his hands and knees to look for a gap in the German wire so that he could get through but was spotted by a sniper and shot through the head. His adjutant, who was with him when he went over, was also killed at some stage in the attack. Hind is commemorated on the Thiepval Memorial; Colonel Wilson, of 5/Sherwood Foresters, is commemorated on the Indian Army (to which he belonged before being transferred to command the battalion) Memorial at Neuve Chapelle.

The brigadier was keen to force the issue by getting men forward, in particular from the support companies of 6/Sherwood Foresters, but insisted that this should only be done under the cover of smoke. This could not be arranged until 3 pm, and was weak and ineffectual. The attack just added to the slaughter and achieved nothing.

Only six of the officers who went into action emerged unscathed. One officer, Lieutenant SE Banwell, was reported missing, believed killed.

Four days afterwards, on July 5th, he crawled into the front line trench completely exhausted and seriously wounded; his

Attack of 46th Division, 1 July 1916.

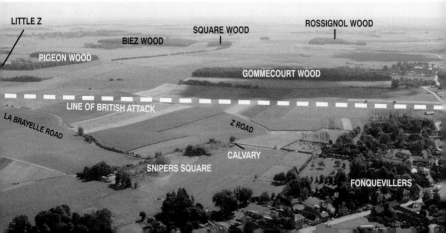

LITTLE Z

PIGEON WOOD

BIEZ WOOD

SQUARE WOOD

ROSSIGNOL WOOD

GOMMECOURT WOOD

LINE OF BRITISH ATTACK

LA BRAYELLE ROAD

Z ROAD

CALVARY

SNIPERS SQUARE

FONQUEVILLERS

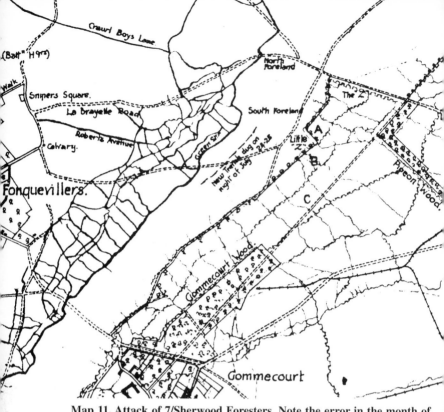

Map 11. Attack of 7/Sherwood Foresters. Note the error in the month of digging of the Jumping Off Trench.

clothing was badly torn. During the time he lay out in No Man's Land he was constantly sniped at by the enemy. He had some seven wounds. During the whole of this time he was without water or food, except that which he was able to procure from the dead around him.

The battalion was relieved early in the morning on 2 July and returned to their billets in Bienvillers. They then moved further out of the line and received a new commanding officer, Lieutenant Colonel Toller, who came from 5/Leicesters. This officer had, in fact, been detailed to go and command a battalion in the 51st (Highland) Division, but was retained by the 46th.

The regimental history of the Robin Hoods puts the failure down to two chief factors - the weather and the wire.

Had the battalion been kept at Sus-St-Leger until within 48 hours of the assault, and then brought fresh and fit for the attack, our chances of success would have been at least 50% greater. The ten days of strenuous labour under such exacting conditions as then prevailed completely undermined the strength and fitness of the battalion. Morning after morning the men returned to their billets in the cellars of Bienvillers, drenched to the skin, with no means of drying their clothing; their rest was continually broken by having to turn out and take shelter in trenches nearby, from heavy enemy shelling.

Although the Robin Hoods were told that the barbed wire entanglements in front of the German trenches would be swept completely away by our artillery fire, only a few odd parties found places where they could force their way through by cutting the wire with special instruments previously fitted to their rifles, and also with ordinary wire cutters - then scrambling through as best they could. This may be explained to some degree, but not to the satisfaction of the attacking battalion, by an entry culled from the German War Diary. 'The wire was unable to withstand the systematic bombardment. Although all damage caused by the

Officers wearing mackintosh capes and rubber boots in an effort to keep dry, which was practically impossible due to the torrential rain and waterlogged trenches.

Lieut.-Col. L A Hind, MC. Killed in action, 1 July 1916, Gommecourt.

bombardment during the day was repaired during the night.'

In fact the attack at this particular point was also the victim of the cunning position of the German line, with flanking fire being brought to fire across almost the width of No Man's Land from the Z and the Little Z. The weather in the days leading up to the attack had had a particularly severe impact on this sector because of the lie of the land; whilst the artillery's fire was hampered by two factors. The first was the soggy ground, which absorbed the impact of many of the shells; the other was technical - the instantaneous fuse was yet to be perfected.

The Officer Commanding 6/North Staffords wrote up an account of the battle afterwards which is to be found in the battalion War Diary.

On the night of Friday June 30th/July 1st the Battalion under command of Major CE Boote marched with 23 officers and 765 OR and took up its dispositions as ordered. [That is from the junction of Leicester Street and the front line inclusive to the junction of Rotten Row and the front line exclusive.] *The attack, which was preceded by an intense bombardment of sixty five minutes, was launched at 7.30 am under cover of smoke. The weather was fine and the breeze favourable for this, but in one part of our lines the man in charge of the smoke was wounded immediately before the smoke was to begin, and as he had no understudy, this portion of the line was*

6/ North Staffs

missed out. The smoke on each side however covered the advance sufficiently. As soon as the smoke started, the enemy opened heavy machine gun fire all along our parapet, and put a strong artillery barrage on our advanced, old front line and retrenchment trenches.

The front line wave advanced at the correct time in a good line, but at once came under such heavy fire that many casualties were suffered before the German line was reached. Here further losses were experienced as the men, being unable to see the gaps cut by our artillery in the German wire, owing to our smoke, ran right on to it, were then hung up, and immediately shot. According to the account of one of our officers the German wire was not well cut and in some of the places where it had been, new wire had been put in. Only about 20 of this wave reached the German front line which they found strongly manned. They were greeted with a hail of bombs, and practically wiped out. The few survivors lay down under the parapet where they remained all day. After dark they managed to crawl back to our lines. Of the four officers who were with this wave, two were killed and two wounded.

The second wave started at the correct distance of 80 yards behind the first. It took them, however, three minutes to get out of our trenches and through our wire. This was owing to the extremely wet and muddy state of our trenches; the mud in the trenches out of which this wave got was from one to two feet deep, and as it was just beginning to dry was very thick and sticky. This was so much so that several men had to be assisted out.

Lieut.-Col. W S N Toller, DSO

The third wave had to get out of the same trench as the second, also took three minutes for the same reason, which made it late, but as the waves in front were going slowly owing to our smoke, which made the advance difficult, their distance from the 2nd wave was not more than 100 yards.

The fourth wave, which started from our retrenchment trench up communication trenches to our old front line and thence over the top laboured under similar difficulties, and having further to go, was not deployed in front of our wire till the third wave was 120 yards in front. The men of this wave carried the bomb carriers and bomb bags, and owing to their weight experienced difficulty in getting out of our trench, and also in getting them through the narrow gaps in our wires.

During the advance, owing to the smoke, waves could not keep the correct distances, and in some parts of the line ran into each other, and became mixed. All these waves had numerous casualties, which included most of the officers and NCOs, and were unable to make much progress. A certain number reached the German wire and front line, where they met with a similar fate to the first wave.

A few men in the smoke mistook our advance trench for the German line, jumped into it and were left behind. A few others

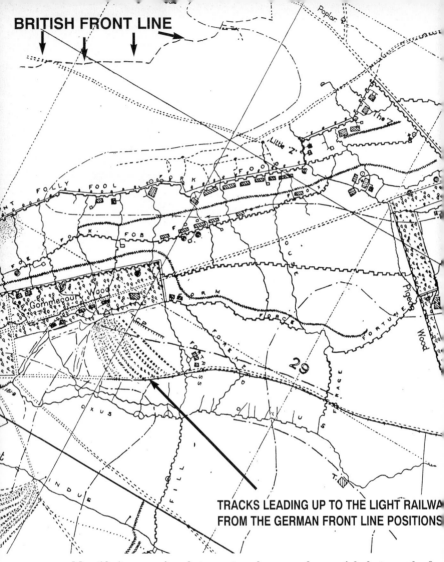

BRITISH FRONT LINE

TRACKS LEADING UP TO THE LIGHT RAILWAY FROM THE GERMAN FRONT LINE POSITIONS

Map 12. A comparison between trench map and an aerial photograph of July 1916. The Z, Little Z and tracks leading to the terminus of the German light railway are all clearly shown.

came back to our old front line under the impression that they had orders to retire. Steps are being taken to try and clear this matter up.

36 men who took part in the attack were a new draft who had never been in a trench before. I will ascertain, as far as possible, what their behaviour was.

I think smoke is an advantage (if thrown well in front of our

Attack Front, 46th Division, Gommecourt, 1 July, 1916.

line) in manoeuvring the waves in position, but should be sent in sufficient time for the view to clear before the actual assault on the German trench made.

Otherwise men cannot see where the German wire is cut and where it is not, and are liable to run right on to the wire and get hung up. The smoke also prevents any observation from the rear. If possible, no wave should have to cross any trench of ours during the attack. Some men are liable to mistake such for the German lines, and others, if the enemy's fire is heavy, are tempted to jump in for cover, and it is difficult to get them on again.

No man of the first four waves at least should carry anything that would prevent him keeping up with the rest of the line or doubling when necessary. A man can carry 4 sandbags, 2 bombs, a bill hook, felling axe, a shovel quite well but not wire, stakes or... (illegible).

6/South Staffords moved up to the line from their billets in Souastre on the evening of 30 June, where they had spent the preceding forty eight hours brought about because of the postponement of the attack. They were to attack on the right of the division, from the Gommecourt road inclusive to the junction of Leicester Street (a CT) and the front line exclusive. They were to advance in line of company (from right to left C, A, B and D) and in four waves with a gap of 80 yards. Each company had a frontage of 75 yards.

6/ South Staffs

The front wave occupied the front line and the others were scattered in the CTs and support lines behind. Unlike their unfortunate comrades in 7/Sherwood Foresters, 6/South Staffords found their trenches to be relatively dry. At about 6.30 am the Germans opened fire with artillery and machine guns. One particular nest, at the north west corner of the village, was very troublesome, but the British artillery proved incapable of knocking it out, and this gun was to cause a lot of casualties when the advance began.

This began at 7.25 am, as the first wave moved forward to an advanced trench under the cover of smoke which provided the same problems here as further to the right. The battalion found that the German wire had indeed been cut, but it had fallen back upon itself and just got entangled again. Only on the left, in a small re-entrant in the German line, was a breakthrough made into the enemy's trenches by D Company as a gap in the wire had been created; and a lodgement was made, for a short while, by the British. C Company had come across Germans in the sucrerie, situated in No Man's Land, but could do almost nothing about them and were stalled by these men.

Within a few minutes the attack was all but over, and the battalion suffered 239 casualties. The German artillery put down three barrage lines - one in No Man's Land, one on the British front line and the third on the communication trenches. The howitzers caused real damage, especially to the Russian saps.

The idea of these saps was to create almost instantaneous communication trenches. They were shallow tunnels dug at right angles to the British line, which could be opened up as necessary and would provide some shelter to troops within them. However the howitzers destroyed many of these.

Shells bursting through the shallow roofs killed those underneath as they worked and left them as if resting on their picks and shovels. The RAMC suffered heavily, complete squads being killed by the explosion of single shells which dropped over the confined spaces whilst they were waiting.

The battalion left the line in the evening of 1 July and moved back to their billets at St Amand.

6/South Staffords' regimental history also provides its explanation for the lack of success, rather different from that of 7/Sherwood Foresters.

In the first place the element of surprise was lacking; this was felt to be so during the final stages of the preparation for attack, and the hope was freely expressed that zero hour would be before

Operation Orders by
Major C.E.Boote
Commanding 1/6th North Staffs Regiment.

Friday, 30th June 1916.

1. Bridges are being placed in a position of readiness in the RETRENCHMENT by the 4th Leicester Regt. These will be placed in position over the Retrenchment after the first three waves have assembled.

2. All bombing and clearing parties and the special carrying party of the 5th North (1 N.C.O. and 10) for the 4th wave as detailed in Appendices "A" and "C", will leave HUMBERCAMP at 5 minutes intervals between parties, commencing at 4.30 p.m. in the following order:-

	Carrying parties -	5th North -	Group 1,
	do	do	2
	do	do	3
	do	do	4
	do	5th South	5
	do	do	6
	Bombing parties	do	
	do	5th North	
	do	6th North	

These parties will proceed by LEICESTER STREET to the Brigade Bomb Store between Leicester Street and Derby Dyke, where they will draw their bombs and proceed to their Assembly trenches.

3. The remainder of the 6th North will assemble in their trenches by waves at 12 midnight, the 3rd wave drawing picks and shovels at the R.E.Dump, E 27 a 3.1 on passing through Fonquevillers. The first two waves assemble in the old front line and the 3rd and 4th waves in the RETRENCHMENT.
At 1 a.m. the 1st wave will move to the new British front line, as detailed in Operation Order No. 65 para 13.

4. Mats for crossing the enemy wire and rod Artillery screens, will be carried by the first wave.
They will be drawn from the R.E.Dump opposite the Town Major's Office.
Any of these articles which are dropped by the first wave in the advance, will be carried on by the 2nd.

5. The 2nd. wave of the 6th North as soon as the smoke is thick enou at "zero" - 3 minutes, will advance up ~~communication trenches~~ *from front line* and through gaps in our wire, deploying as soon as possible.

6. A smoke barrage will be formed, produced from the old front line, "P" grenades being thrown into the wire.

7. All ranks will be warned against allowing bayonets to show over the parapet.
Silence will be preserved during and after the assembly in the trenches.

8. Nos. 1 and 2 Saps will be opened tonight. The O.C. 6th North will post sentry on No. 2 Sap to ensure that no one but the 1st Monmouth Regt working parties, enters the sap until the work is completed.
The continuation of the saps etc. will be carried out as detailed in Operation Orders No. 65 para. 15.

9. All four main communication trenches, NOTTINGHAM STREET, DERBY DYKE, LEICESTER STREET, and LINCOLN LANE will be used as "UP" communication trenches until 3 a.m. after which hour DERBY DYKE and LINCOLN LANE will become "DOWN" trenches. only.

10. 2nd. 3rd. and 4th waves will parade by waves at 8 p.m. ready to march off.
Head of column to be at point where Railway crosses St. AMAND road, order of march, "C" "D" "B" "A"
They will march via SOUASTRE and "C" Track.

11. O.C. Companies will report personally *to Bgdr Ballee 1/6th* when their Companies are in their proper positions in the trenches.

12. The only Officers, N.C.O's and men excused parade will be
Lieut. Turner,
2nd. Lieut. Fisher,
3 N.C.O's per Company already detailed
(This includes C.Q.M.S. who will return after issuing stores)
These will live at LA BEZIQUE FARM.
Cook Sergt and 4 Cooks,
Q.M. Staff,
Orderly Room Sergt and Pte Waters.

(sd) F.R.STUART SHAW, Lieut.,
Adjutant, 1/6th North Staffordshire Regiment.
30-6-1916.

dawn, in order that the objective could be approached unseen. [In fact the French determined the hour of attack, for reasons that were perfectly sound, at least to their much more battle experienced army, and they had a very successful first day.] *The expedient of turning day into night by means of smoke bombs placed the attacking troops at a disadvantage which was not shared by the enemy. It appeared that the artillery preparation was based upon the theory that the front line of the enemy trenches was lightly held, and that his main strength lay in the support line. Although our field guns paid great attention to the wire, our heavier guns were more concerned with the support line, and other defensive features. In point of fact the front line was immensely strong. There were ample deep dugouts, well provided with exits, in which the enemy could shelter with complete immunity, and from which he emerged on hearing the whistle of the sentries. The only means of ensuring success would have been to obliterate the front line of the German trenches, and so make sure of that objective; but this would have required all our guns, and might have precluded the possibility of capturing further objectives which were essential to the larger plan of operations. It must also be remembered that the use of the creeping barrage had not yet been adopted.*

The battalion had a chance to view things from the German perspective when the Germans withdrew from Gommecourt in 1917, when once again the 46th Division was in the sector.

On looking back towards our lines we then saw what command of the ground he had possessed in this ideal position for defence. Machine gun emplacements, strengthened with concrete, so as to be impervious to any but the heaviest shells, gave him an oblique fire across his front, and the emplacement of the gun which had given us so much trouble prior to the attack was found to be almost untouched, despite the special efforts of our artillery to demolish it.

5/ North Staffs

5/North Staffords were in immediate support of 6/North Staffords, in turn on the left of 6/South Staffords. 5/North Staffords were completely overwhelmed by the German barrage which came down as the advance commenced - in particular those who were in the

Panorama of the 46 Division front from the Z.

GOMMECOURT WOOD MILITARY CEMETERY

GOMMECOURT WOOD

Z ROAD

Little Z

German Front Line

The Z

communication trenches, and only a few men from the battalion got close to the German front line. One of these was Lance Corporal R Tivey.

We went over in broad daylight and in full view of the enemy lines. Attached to my wave would be some twenty five men. We mounted all together, keeping extended order line, about two yards' interval, and set off at an easy pace for the next trench. After having proceeded no more than 20 paces, the whole line fell as one man, leaving me running, whereupon I was struck for the first time and fell. I did not know what had happened really, and surmised that the line had been wiped out, since deliberate rifle fire and maxim fire was concentrated on us. I crawled some yards left, but my wound was not bad enough to permit of returning, so I rose again, and ran in quarter circles for the enemy trench. This time shrapnel was bursting, and I was the centre of fire. A bullet grazed my thumb, and I lost my rifle, another hitting my shrapnel helmet.

When within some ten or twenty yards of the enemy barbed wire, I was struck again, doubling me up. Close by was a shell hole, into which I crawled, the Germans shooting at me when I was down, and hitting the sole of my boot. They turned the maxim on me, and sniped at me if I made a movement. Heavy crumps and mortars were bursting all around. That I did not go mad is more than I can explain away, but I kept remarkably cool. After 12 hours of it, I crawled out, under cover of dark, and made my way back. This was difficult, since my wounds had caught me in the back and the stomach, and I was bent nearly double.

The officer commanding A Company, Captain JG Worthington, gave an account from his perspective, here edited.

A Company was in reserve, and, after providing a party to be attached to the machine gunners as carriers, trench wardens [or Battle Police], storemen, and various other details, it found itself reduced to less than fifty men, and a few odds and ends left over from D Company.

The orders were that at four minutes to Zero the men in every line except those in the advanced trench were to turn to their right, and file up the first communication trench until they

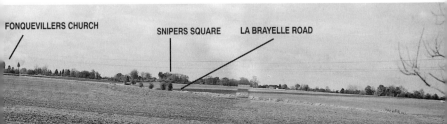

FONQUEVILLERS CHURCH   SNIPERS SQUARE   LA BRAYELLE ROAD

Behind the ruined remains of some of Gommecourt's cottages lies Gommecourt Wood.

reached the front line. They were there to deploy and follow the preceding line over the top. My orders were, to commence moving forward from the village (ie Fonquevillers) at that time, place my men in the support line and then report to battalion headquarters.

The final bombardment commenced at 6 am and was very severe; the noise in the village being terrific. The journey up the communication trench was not exactly pleasant, as the enemy was pitching his shells very accurately and I had several casualties, including one sergeant killed. The majority reached the support line, and I proceeded to make my way forward with a runner. After going a short distance I found the trench blocked by a small party of (5th) Leicesters. The rear man told me that their Colonel was in front, and that they were unable to go on, as the attack had been held up. Another party of Leicesters came up behind us. Shells were dropping all round, and an officer and sergeant major of the party behind were killed.

I managed to reach Colonel Jones of the 5/Leicesters, and together we made our way forward over dead and dying bodies and wire entanglements that had been dropped by the carrying parties, until we reached an assembly trench a short distance in rear of the front line.

Gommecourt village photographed in the 1930s.

Artistic dramatisation of the attack on Gommecourt, where the advancing troops were cut down by the German machine guns.

I went forward to my battalion headquarters, and found Colonel Burnett at the telephone, speaking to the Brigadier, who told him that he must reorganise the attack and push on. He then announced that he was going out to see what was going on, and told me to remain where I was.

After the Colonel had been gone a short while the Brigadier asked for him on the telephone, and several runners were sent out to find him, but failed to do so. It afterwards transpired that he had been mortally wounded. [He is buried at Warlincourt Halte British Cemetery, Saulty; 6/North Staffords lost their commanding officer, Lieutenant Colonel CE Boote, as well; he is buried in Gommecourt Wood Cemetery.] *The Brigadier then told me to get into touch with the colonel of 5/South Staffords, reorganise, and attack again at 3.30 in the afternoon, in co-operation with the 5/South Staffords on the right and the 6/Sherwood Foresters on the left. At this moment Major Wenger*

A German machine gun team. Well sited and manned machine guns would cause tremendous casualties in the attack.

arrived, and took over the command. By his orders I went out and proceeded with the work of the reorganisation, which consisted in sorting out the men of the three battalions, 5th and 6th North and Leicesters, who were all mixed up. The 5th North were collected in the front line, the Leicesters in the Assembly trench in rear, and the 6th North in the support line. By the time some kind of order had been established it was well on in the afternoon, the weather was very hot, and the men were exhausted.

We were told that we were to wait for a smoke barrage before attempting to advance. Shortly before 3.30 pm a few puffs of smoke were seen, and the enemy immediately put down a shrapnel barrage, and we were about to attack when an order arrived from the brigade that we were to stand fast.

Thus saved from a futile gesture, the battalion was removed to Bailleulmont, having lost seven officers killed and five wounded and suffering about 300 casualties amongst the other ranks.

5/Leicesters were attached to 137 Brigade for the attack. Two platoons were detailed off to dig a trench from the sucrerie in the wake of the attacking battalions, and indeed started their task, getting so far as to mark out the trench. However the job was impossible, and after sustaining a number of casualties the party was ordered back to the British line.

The decision to reorganise for another attack was not as senseless as it might seem, because it was still far from clear how successful the 56th Division had been, and it was essential to ensure that they were not left stranded; the operation would have failed, and the 56th might well be cut off if they had managed to complete their task.

Our lines, hopelessly sticky from the bad weather, were now congested with dead and wounded; the communication trenches were jammed with stretcher cases and parties coming in, the up and down rules were not observed and, above all, the enemy's artillery enfiladed the front line from the north, the communications from the east...There was also another serious difficulty to reorganisation. The men were too well trained in their particular duties. A private soldier who has been told every day for a month that his one duty will be to carry a box of bombs to point Q, cannot readily forget that, and take an efficient part in an unrehearsed attack.

When the order came through to abandon the proposed attack, the Staffords were ordered out of the line and the Leicesters took their place.

The rest of the night and the following day were spent in collecting the dead and wounded from our lines, from the newly dug and now water-logged assembly trench in front, and from No Man's Land...The next day was spent in the same way, and by the evening the trenches had been considerably tidied up, when at 9 pm we were relieved by the Rangers and marched back to Bienvillers au Bois.

The two Lincolns battalions came out of the day comparatively lightly; 4/Lincolns occupied the part of the 46th Division line that flanked the north west part of Gommecourt Park, and which was not to be attacked. The battalion moved into their part of the line during the night of 27 June; unlike other battalions which were withdrawn when the attack was postponed forty eight hours, they remained in their trenches. They also aimed to keep the Germans on the alert, an example of which was the patrol sent out on the night of the 29th.

The battalion sent out a raiding party consisting of thirty four other ranks under Lieutenant CN Bond and Second Lieutenants E Elliott and Quantrail. The raiders reached the enemy's wire, but were then discovered by German listening posts. Hostile troops swarmed out of the trenches and attempted to surround the Lincolns, but were stopped by rifle fire and bombs. For an hour there was a desperate fight in No Man's Land, but at 12.30 am the signal for withdrawal was given. Lieutenant Bond was wounded in the neck and died on the way to the dressing station: one other rank was slightly wounded. [Bond is buried in

Fonquevillers Military Cemetery.]

The battalion's role for the attack, apart from patrolling, was not passive. Whilst men in other brigades made their way to their assault positions, the whole battalion, with the exception of the Lewis gun teams, went out into No Man's Land and set about digging a false jumping off trench in front of the British wire. This work was made as conspicuous as possible, particularly the parapet, even though the end result was only a very shallow affair; within a little over three hours the battalion was back in its trenches. Apart from holding the line on the day, the battalion took no active part in the attack and suffered relatively very minor casualties.

5/Lincolns were in reserve and moved to the northern part of Midland Trench during the morning of 1 July. At 8.30 pm the CO was ordered to send officers up to reconnoitre the German front before 137 Brigade; at this stage it was still thought that there were elements of 139 Brigade (on the left) holding out in the German lines. The Lincolns were ordered to attack at 11 pm and try and establish contact with the Sherwood Foresters and to establish themselves in the German lines. Command in 6/Sherwood Foresters was as difficult as with the 7th, for they too had lost their commanding officer in the attack.

At 9.30 pm the battalion moved forward from Midland Trench, but their progress was slowed by the appalling conditions in the communication trenches, what there was left of them. Thus orders to company commanders were only given out at 11 pm. All companies were to attack and they were got out into No Man's Land. Orders were then changed, so that now the battalion was only to make contact with any remaining Sherwood Foresters and bring them back. At midnight the forward platoons went off, but lost contact with each other in the dark and only two platoons made it to the wire, which was uncut. The Germans spotted them, and a veritable firework display of flares and Verey lights lit up the whole sector. The men had no alternative but to lie down. The Brigadier was informed of the hopelessness of the situation, but the Divisional commander insisted that the attack must continue; time was taken for this to be reorganised, but before it could be launched it was cancelled and the battalion withdrew back to the British front line. Fortunately this meant that casualties were relatively light - three officers and forty five other ranks. The battalion remained

The German line ran along the forward edge of Gommecourt Park.

GOMMECOURT WOOD CEMETERY

in the line until 3 July.

There was little of consolation to find in the attacks on the 46th Division front on 1 July apart from acts of heroism.[2]

The Aftermath: Gommecourt Revisited.

In fact the 46th Division were to have another visit to their old 1 July battlefield - almost covering the same area - but this time with a far happier outcome, as they followed the withdrawing Germans as they made their way back to the Hindenburg Line in the early months of 1917.

The Division moved to the Monchy au Bois sector at the beginning of December 1916, having enjoyed a 'rest' in the rear areas for some five weeks. Time was taken to relax, bathe, wash clothes and to get away from the sound of the guns. However there were also lots of ceremonial parades and field exercises, as 4/Leicesters history describes.

One of the flies in the ointment was the distance of the training area from billets and the time wasted getting there. Ceremonial drill and open order attacks were the order of the day, and neither exercise is easy. The battalion had much to learn, and there was a lot of 'as you were-ing' and 'do it again'. And sometimes, when standing rigidly to attention not daring to move a muscle, or when lying prone in the dampest part of a muddy field, the thought flashed through the patient brain of Private Atkins that there were certain advantages to be gained by living in a secluded little fire bay in a front line trench. Officers are not so particular, or NCOs so officious within two hundred yards of the enemy.

The Robin Hoods (7/Sherwood Foresters) also did time in the sector, moving to Souastre and then Fonquevillers.

Souastre was separated from Fonquevillers by about four miles of undulating mud flats, scored with disused gun pits, across which ran a straight and melancholy road. The oily surface of the plain was pitted with an infinity of round pools of every diameter; and a shattered line of tree stumps festooned with broken telephone wires, which marked the road, was the only feature to break the monotony of mud. The two villages were in perfect harmony with the rest of the picture. Both were in the last stage of dissolution. Souastre still boasted some houses with

4/Lincolns position – looking towards Gommecourt Wood Military Cemetery.

ground floor rooms intact. Fonquevillers consisted of a few cellars, liberally covered with debris. From one such pile half covering a ragged and noisome hole projected a large notice informing the world that the Town Major of Fonquevillers lived below! This hapless individual spent a precarious existence in keeping up a census of available holes technically known as a 'list of billets'.

With the winter, the remnants of the trees in the wood opposite had lost their leafs. The strength of the enemy position was apparent - the Little Z and the Z and then the five lines of German trenches rising one above each other, tiered, on the rising ground. The British trenches were also in a horrendous state. Systematic efforts had been made over the summer and autumn months to improve them. Sump holes had been dug and in particularly bad places the trenches had boarded floors on piles. However even these were well under water, and in any case the wooden coverings had often rotted or floated away - thereby creating considerable possibilities for the unsuspecting soldier to get a dousing.

See map/photo 88-89

For the first few weeks in this line the British were short of heavy trench mortars, and the Germans were able to use theirs with relative impunity. A particularly irritating piece of impudence had been the habit of the driver of the train of a German light railway to blow the engine whistle as he returned home after delivering stores during the night. This light railway ran up to the German battalion headquarters just north of Oxus on the road from Gommecourt that runs behind Gommecourt Wood towards La Brayelle Farm. The arrival of new mortars, the 'flying pig', put this terminus, at long last, within range of British fire.

The night after the charges had arrived the impudent Boche again blew his whistle, and was rewarded by a flying pig all to himself; and it was noticed with satisfaction that the practice of whistling on trench railways was discontinued from that night.

Having spent an enjoyable Christmas in billets (though half in Souastre and half in Fonquevillers), the battalion was back in the line on Boxing Day; in the early hours of 28 December they faced a raid.

It was a well conceived raid, for the enemy's barrage never quite lifted from our line. The isolated forward posts, taking what cover the battered trench afforded, noticed its weakening and saw the enemy already in the wire. He appeared in great strength before our Lewis gun post, offering a splendid target. But the gun had been damaged in the barrage and the little party had to rely on their rifles. The fight was short and sharp. The enemy was repulsed, but not before Lieutenant Barnes, who had taken command of the post, had fallen mortally wounded by a German bomb.

The time in the trenches were generally quiet, with tedium relieved by trying to entice one of the thousands of rats to take the bait of a piece of cheese on the end of a bayonet and then be blasted by pulling the trigger, or by watching some of the numerous aerial combats in the sky above. In the New Year for some weeks there was a particularly hard frost. There was the surprising sensation of being completely dry. Work on the trenches became impossible, as the ground became as iron. The moonlit nights made the night almost as day, and the sentries were further assisted by the sprinkling of snow. Patrolling became more comfortable - but also more dangerous, as it was so much easier to spot people in No Man's Land.

To obviate the latter difficulty we were issued with voluminous white capes and cowls. This traditional form of camouflage gave us considerable protection and still more amusement. Not only had they a most hideous effect on our personal appearances, but they were somewhat ill adapted to stealthy movement. The sight of an austere and monk-like figure erect in the moonlight, clasping a Lewis gun in one arm, and with the other striving to disentangle his priestly robes from the barbed wire, was enough to enliven the coldest night

On 14 February rumours began to circulate that the Germans were withdrawing, and once more optimistic talk spread about the possibility of being in Berlin for the summer. However, the Germans were not going anywhere without a fight. Thus at 3 am on 21 February, 4/Leicesters had a raid inflicted upon them.

The enemy then put down a heavy barrage, and it looked very much as though they were going to make a raid. Three platoons occupying the front line withdrew or thinned their line and blocked the communication trenches but left Lewis guns to hold the front line in case of attack. At the same time they asked for artillery support, and in less than four minutes all our guns in

> *the neighbourhood were plastering Gommecourt. It was an unpleasant hour and a half. If the Germans intended a raid none of them reached our line.*

The German actions here were typical of other parts of the line from which they were preparing to withdraw; they maintained an offensive posture right up to the last moment, and even when the time had come to pull back to the Hindenburg Line, some fifteen to twenty kilometres behind their positions, they did so gradually and frequently counter-attacked at local level so that the following British troops had to proceed with great caution.

At midnight on 24/25 February the Brigadier had reason to believe that the Boche was going to leave his lines. A strong patrol was sent out, cut gaps in the wire, but found the Germans still in occupation. 5/Leicesters noted,

> *At dawn it was very foggy, and there was some shouting heard in Gommecourt, which sounded like 'Bonsoir', but at 7.10 am the enemy opened a heavy bombardment which lasted three and a half hours. Shells of every kind were fired and our trenches hit in several places; one man was killed. The next night patrols were out again and, though it was found that the Boche had evacuated Gommecourt Park, he was still in the village, where the following morning dugouts were seen to be on fire. Wire was cut and everything prepared for the advance.*

The Germans remained in his line; and 5/Leicesters withdrew to Souastre to be replaced by 4/Leicesters.

On 27 February men of the battalion began their cautious advance into the village; that night some four hundred yards of the German front in a semicircle to the west of the village were occupied; this was taken forward another two hundred yards, and then under cover of mist, at 8 am, another five hundred yards. Thus by 1 March the old German third line was more or less occupied, along with the communication trenches, in the immediate vicinity of the village.

> *It had been a good show. The enemy had evacuated some trenches and had been bombed out of others. No Man's Land had been crossed without a casualty. And what a place No Man's Land was! The dead of the attack of 1 July were still lying out just where they had fallen eight months previously, and arms and equipment lay all over the place.*

When 5/Leicesters returned to the line on 1 March, they were now in position to the east of Gommecourt, though the Germans were very much in evidence in both the Z and Pigeon Wood, as well as in the village itself and in Gommecourt Wood. This latter occupation became very obvious to the Divisional Commander of the Royal Artillery, Brigadier General Campbell,

> 'he went into the wood [Gommecourt], *thinking it unoccupied, and was chased out by a fat Boche throwing potato mashers* [German hand grenades]'.

The battalion steadily moved forward, and indeed went into the deep dugouts that were connected with each other, right out to the Z. These tunnels post dated the 1 July attack; the report on the battle had strongly recommended that the German dugouts should be interconnected by tunnel, because so many of them had become potential tombs when both their entrances had been blown in during the British bombardment. It did mean that the Germans sat at one end, whilst British troops sat at the other of the same tunnel. The battalion also came across the massive number of booby traps that the Germans had left behind them - loose boards exploding a bomb when trodden upon, trip wires at the bottom of dugout steps bringing down the roof, braziers with bombs in their contents, waiting to be lit and so forth. However, the battalions had been warned of these things and suffered no casualties.

On 2 March the battalion continued to push back the Germans, fanning out in a semicircle from Gommecourt Church and clearing about a nine hundred yard front; by the time that they returned to the line on 11 March the Germans had withdrawn beyond the area attacked by the division in July 1916.

On 3 March the Robin Hoods found themselves in the trenches before Fonquevillers, with the right on Roberts Avenue. 8/Sherwood Foresters was on the right, but positioned in Gommecourt Wood, so

The right of the 46th Division attack and Gommecourt village.

SITE OF THE QUADRILATERAL

GOMMECOURT WOOD

GOMMECOURT WOOD CEMETERY

PORTION of GERMAN DUGOUT.

Shewing Reinforced Concrete over Entrance and Periscope Shaft.

(From Plan captured July 1916)

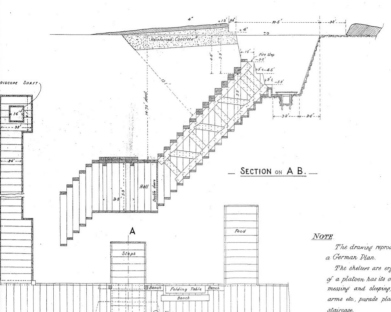

_ SECTION ON A B. _

NOTE

    The drawing reproduced is only a po
a German Plan.

    The shelters are organized so that ea
of a platoon has its own accommodation
messing and sleeping, shelves and rack
arms etc, parade place in the passage
staircase.

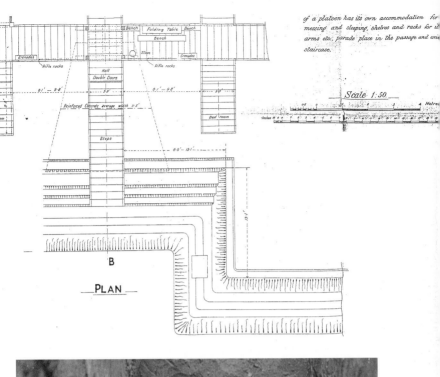

of a platoon has its own accommodation for
messing and sleeping, shelves and racks for it
arms etc, parade place in the passage and exi
staircase.

Scale 1:50

B

PLAN

that the line formed an awkward kink. The Robin Hoods were in the old trenches, and then there was a gap of several hundred yards to the 8th's left flank. Sticking out from the German line was the infamous Z; the intervening distance between the two British lines had to be policed by aggressive and frequent patrolling. This state of affairs only lasted a very short while, as on 8 March the Robin Hoods entered the Z just as the Germans were leaving.

The Germans, as they withdrew, made a point of destroying and laying waste as much of the countryside, water supplies, roads and habitations as possible. The Robin Hoods followed the Germans as they moved on beyond Biez Wood and towards Bucquoy; the problems were considerable, especially as the severe weather had broken.

The lines held were either mere groups of shell holes or portions of old German trenches, water logged and impassable. With the breaking of the frost the whole country had again become a vast morass, and movement along the trenches even where they existed was quite impossible. The only way of getting about was over the top, and the difficulty of finding the way, especially by night, over a strange and shell-pitted country almost entirely devoid of landmarks, was often insoluble. We tried to mark out tracks by tape, but these speedily disappeared in the mud. A partial solution was the erection of small landmarks at intervals of some hundred yards. The direction from one to the other had to be learnt by long and bitter

German gun smashed by the British bombardment.

Investigating a newly captured German dugout.

experience. A German billican stuck on a rifle is not a conspicuous object at the best of times. To strike it on a dark night across some hundred yards of mud, over which it was impossible to walk, even for a few paces, in a straight line was a nightly trial, which many who were there on battalion Headquarters have good cause to remember.

It was also a sombre time for another reason. The Robin Hoods, along with the other battalions of the division, took the opportunity of searching for the bodies of those who had been killed in the action on 1 July. The bodies of four of their officers were found on the still uncut wire in front of the wood, where they had fallen in the assault, and they

The Germans carried out a plan of utter destruction in the areas which lay between their original front line and their new trenches to which they retired in March 1917. This dreary landscape shown in the photograph below was typical of the scene that met the eyes of the advancing British troops.

In the foreground of this photograph is a German gun which is being used by the British to shell the German lines as they retreat towards Bapaume.
TAYLOR LIBRARY

were brought in and buried in Fonquevillers Military Cemtery - Captains Leman and Walker and Second Lieutenants Flint and Gamble; there was no trace of the others.

By 22 March 1917 the division was finally rid of Gommecourt and its surroundings.

1. WO95/2685
2. Sources for this chapter are the same as for that preceding it.

A smouldering street in Bapaume, a few hours after it was captured for the first time in the German retreat of March 1917. TAYLOR LIBRARY

Chapter Five

THE ATTACK: THE GERMAN VIEW

The Germans, like the British, split the area they held into sectors; the 55th Reserve Infantry Regiment held most of the line opposite the two British divisions. From north to south they split the line into five sectors, from G1 and G2 in the north (effectively opposite 46th Division, with G2 being south west of the sunken road), G3 centred on the Kern Redoubt and G4 to the junction between Eel and Fight and Firm and G5 to the junction of Ferret and Ems. To the regiment's right was the 91st Reserve Infantry Regiment and to the left was the 170th Infantry Regiment.

The first item that the War Diary of the 55th reported was the new trench dug on the night of 23 June on 139 Brigade front. Thereafter, and for the next few days, the reports largely relate to the effect of the British bombardment. Thus on 24 June,

6.30 am Heavy continuous shrapnel fire on Sectors G1 and G2, which increased to an intense bombardment towards midday. Some medium shells on G2. Casualties: 1 other rank wounded

The shelling is disruptive. The report for 25 June says,

During the night continuous shrapnel fire on all approach roads and the area in the rear. Heavy artillery fire on the whole sector, increasing in intensity.

Germans at Courcelles-le-Comte in July 1916, boarding trucks to move up to the German front line at Gommecourt.

Germans pass the time, in the relative safety of their dugouts and trenches, before the bombardment begins.

8.45 am The officer commanding G Right Sector [ie opposite 46th Division] *reports heavy fire on his trenches. Patrol reports cannot be forwarded owing to the danger of losing the runners. Sent later by telephone.*

Yet by 10 am the casualties merely consisted of one dead, one seriously wounded and one wounded. Despite a day when all sorts of artillery and trench mortars were brought to bear on the village and area, and despite frequent bursts of machine gun fire and despite 12th Company losing its cooker to a direct hit, the casualty list for the day was only one killed and eleven wounded.

Life continued, bearable in the deep dugouts. Reinforcements were received - 165 men arrived on the 26th; gas clouds were reported; one of the batteries in Biez Wood, about fourteen hundred yards east of Gommecourt, reported several direct hits; every so often a dugout was badly damaged and the Royal Flying Corps maintained an irritating presence in the skies above the village. But the men were also on edge,

Maxim gun arranged for air defence. This image clearly illustrates the equipment which caused terrible carnage to the British army as they attempted to reach the German lines. TAYLOR LIBRARY

Gommecourt April 1916.

despite the bland language of the diarist. At 3 am on 27 June,

> *The Brigade reports that an English attack will take place at 4 am - unknown whether English or German time meant* [yes, we were out of sync with Europe even then!]. *170th Regiment reports English prisoner's statement that an attack will take place at 4.55 am. 3rd Battalion ordered to stand to.*

Nothing happened, as we know, but at 5.50 am the diary records,

> *G Right reports wire south of the Gommecourt-Fonquevillers road still in good condition;* [this part of the line was not to be attacked; this would be the sort of evidence that German intelligence officers would be examining] *also the English wire. North of the road fifty yards of the English wire has been removed. Our wire in front of G1 damaged.*

Machine gun position in Gommecourt, October 1916.

The diary goes on to report the fact that the linesmen for the telephones are usually able to keep them operational. Casualties remain negligible, but damage from heavy artillery (in particular 15 inch shells) were causing trouble, with more dugouts being blown in, a heavy trench mortar being destroyed (the other being removed to a reserve emplacement) and trenches, especially in G1, being rendered impassable. It is worth noting here that these heavy shells were particularly lacking in the British army at this time - indeed one of the causes traditionally given for the failure of the attacks on 1 July was the shortage of heavy calibre artillery. The French had far more of it, and some of this was made available to the British in the south, areas where the most complete success was obtained on 1 July.

On 30 June, in the morning, the War Diary reported that, *'the impression of an attack on Gommecourt being imminent is not confirmed from the right sector'*, whilst the interrogation of a prisoner was recorded at 2.30 pm which revealed that no black troops were present. Why this question was asked (it is unlikely to have been volunteered as a statement) is open to conjecture, but the Germans held a popular belief that these troops were not too fussy about how they dealt with their prisoners; though there is no factual evidence that black troops were any more brutal in this regard than anyone else. The only ones the British had were members of the British West Indies Regiment, and the infantry were mainly white or mixed race, so presumably it referred to troops from the Indian Army, and there were no infantry in France.

The total casualties suffered by the regiment before the opening of the attack were few - six killed and forty four wounded, a tribute to the strength of the German defences, and the lack of British heavy artillery.

Saturday July 1st 1916. The intense bombardment shortly before the attack succeeded in rendering the front trenches in G1 and G5 ripe for assault. The enemy attained this by

Gommecourt, October 1916.

concentrating a very great proportion of his artillery and trench mortars (up to the largest calibres) against these sectors. It was then evident that the main attack would be directed north and south of Gommecourt village in order to cut off the garrison of Gommecourt.

G1 Sector [46th Division]

7.30 am. An extremely violent bombardment began, overwhelming all the trenches and sweeping away the wire.

8.30 am. The enemy's fire lifted (note German time was one hour ahead of British time). The enemy's attack, which was made under cover of gas bombs (in fact smoke) was perceived...The shell holes were occupied exactly at the right moment and the attackers were received with hand-grenades. The barrage fire which was called for began at once.

8.40 am. Strong hostile skirmishing line deployed from opposite G1. They were at once met by heavy machine gun and infantry fire.

See maps on pages 75 and 127

Reinforcements rushed across from the third line to assist their comrades in the front line, these arriving 'at the decisive time'. Despite the determined efforts of the enemy they were repulsed everywhere. Members of 4 Company (holding the front line) were particularly effective, some of whom, 'sprang forward with a cheer and threw their grenades'.

10.30 am. The fine spirit of the brave troops of the 2nd and 4th Companies succeeded by their stubborn resistance in annihilating the thick charging waves of the English. The ground was covered with numbers of dead, and in front of our trench lay quantities of English arms and equipment. Gradually the artillery fire recommenced on the front line trenches and rose to a pitch of extreme violence in the course of the afternoon. The fact that all attacks were completely repulsed without the enemy gaining a footing in the front line of G1 at any point is due, next to the bravery of the troops, to the carefully thought out arrangements of Major von Bothmer (the battalion commander).

The story in this sector is comparatively brief; but that on G5, opposite the 56th Division, is considerably more complex.

See map page 28

G5 Sector.

6.30 am. Intense bombardment of all calibres up to 15 inch commenced against G5 with the result that most of the entrances to the dugouts were blown in, the trenches were flattened out and the wire was destroyed. The front trench was enfiladed from the

114

ng (other ranks) :

7th Company	.	.	.	14
8th Company	.	.	.	22
11th Company	.	.	.	2
Total	.	.	.	38

APPENDIX III

ITION EXPENDITURE DURING THE PERIOD JUNE 24TH TO LY 1ST, 1916, BY THE ARTILLERY OF THE 2ND GUARD RES. VISION

Date.	60 Field Guns and Hows.			20 Heavy Guns and Hows.					
	Field Guns 40.	Light Field Hows. 12.	9-cm. Guns 8.	10-cm. Guns '14 2.	15-cm. How. '96 4.	15-cm. How. '02/13 8.	Russian 15-cm. Guns 4.	21-cm. How. (old pattern) 2.	
ne .	528	223	211	8	80	138	42	17	
.	1,105	313	452	214	173	357	154	102	
.	3,806	621	651	385	79	953	74	67	
.	4,518	468	208	70	152	664	260	68	
.	664	210	173	—	38	404	39	32	
.	751	69	108	126	141	247	67	6	
.	548	90	—	—	31	25	52	—	
.	11,683	4,429	2,070	609	481	2,821	258	252	
al .	23,603	6,423	3,873	1,412	1,175	5,609	946	544	

German statistics from the action at Gommecourt. Notice how few casualties were caused by the preparatory bombardment.

APPENDIX I

DISTRIBUTION OF THE 55TH RES. INFANTRY REGIMENT ON JULY 1ST

	G. LEFT (2ND BATT.) Sector Commander : Captain Minck.			G. RIGHT (1ST BATT.) Sector Commander : Major V. Bothmer.	
	G. 5.	G. 4.	G. 3.	G. 2.	G. 1.
Front Line :	8th Coy. 170 Rifles. 3 M.G's.	6th Coy. 134 Rifles.	5th Coy. 171 Rifles. 1 M.G	3rd Coy. 137 Rifles. 2 M.G's.	4th Coy. 126 Rifles. 2 M.G's.
Close Support :	8th Coy.	6th Coy. 26 Rifles.	5th Coy. 1 M.G	3rd Coy. 12 Rifles.	4th Coy. 18 Rifles.
Kern Redoubt :	7th Coy. 158 Rifles. 2 M.G's.	Inf. Pioneer Coy. 150 Rifles.		1st Coy. 159 Rifles. 1 M.G	2nd Coy. 90 Rifles.
1st Switch Line :		10th Coy. 62 Rifles.		2nd Coy. 62 Rifles.	
2nd Switch Line :			10th Coy. 100 Rifles.		
Intermediate Line :	...2.4 ...		M.G.		
Resting :	9th and 12th Coys. in Brigade Reserve. 11th Coy., Regimental Reserve. In Bucquoy, 14 M.G's. and remainder of Inf. Pioneer Coy.				

Thus the front line was held with 738 rifles and 8 M.G's., with 56 rifles and 1 M.G. in close support.

The Kern Redoubt was held with 557 rifles and 3 M.G's.

APPENDIX II

CASUALTIES OF THE 55TH RES. INFANTRY REGIMENT FOR THE PERIOD JUNE 24TH TO JULY 2ND, 1916

Date.	Officers.			Other ranks.		
	Killed.	Wounded.	Missing.	Killed.	Wounded.	Missing.
24th June, 1916 .	—	—	—	—	1	—
25th ,,	—	—	—	1	11	—
26th ,,	—	—	—	1	10	—
27th ,,	—	—	—	3	4	—
28th ,,	—	—	—	—	3	—
29th ,,	—	—	—	—	4	—
30th ,,	—	—	—	1	11	—
1st July, 1916 .	1	5	—	109	244	38
2nd ,,	—	—	—	—	8	—
Total .	1	5	—	115	296	38
		6			449	

direction of *Fonquevillers. Every round from the British guns pitched in the trench, thus rendering its occupation, even by detached posts, impossible.*

7.30 am. [A battery observer reported that] *The enemy has overrun sectors N1 and N2* [ie attacked by the London Scottish, Rangers and QVRs] *and has pushed between Süd* [Exe] *Trench and Roth Trench, beyond Gommecourt Cemetery as far as the beginning of the 1st Guard Line and the Kern Redoubt.*

The enemy's bombardment lifted on to the Kern Redoubt and the first switch line. Directly afterwards, under cover of smoke clouds, the enemy's assault began. On the left flank of G4 and the right flank of G5 [ie along Firm] *the assault was completely repulsed, but in the meantime two platoons in G5 were overrun by the attack, the garrison not having been able to leave the dugouts in time owing to the entrance having been blown in.* [The 8th Company] *was only able to beat off the attacks of the succeeding lines which advanced from Patrol Wood* [to the north east of the Cemetery], *and to block a further advance, without being able to counter attack the enemy who had already penetrated the front line.*

The enemy forces which had penetrated into N1 and N2 were held up and driven back to Gommecourt Cemetery after a heavy bombing encounter with members of the Kern Redoubt garrison.

7.40 am. (7 Company, left of Kern Redoubt, was ordered to) attack the enemy who has penetrated into G5 and the sector of the 8th Company. The attack will be made through Süd Trench. The attack could not be carried out this order at once, but prevented the enemy's further advance, which was held up about 100 yards south of the Kern Redoubt between Hauser (Eel) and Süd (Exe)Trenches on a front of 100 yards, where he had dug himself in and brought up two machine guns. The enemy, who was amply supplied with machine guns and every form of equipment for close fighting, offered a stubborn resistance. His exact strength could not be ascertained, but he was known to be everywhere in far superior numbers. [This of course, in this part of the battlefield, was far from true.] *All telephonic communications had been destroyed in the bombardment, and even the cable, buried two metres deep, had been cut. The Regimental* [British equivalent, Brigade] *Headquarters were thus without news of the progress of events.*

The Germans decided to bring on the reserve battalion from its billets in Bucquoy, reinforced with elements of the 170th Regiment. The battalion commander, Major Tauscher, moved to Hill 147 at 11 am to observe the battle - this is situated in the German Intermediate Line to

German reserve battalion in Bucquoy, July 1916.

the north east of Rossignol Wood. He could see that the British were continuing their push northwards into Felon and had secured the east flank of G5. He ordered a company to attack along Roth (Ems) and another along Lehmann (Etch); he could see that these trenches, plus Becker (Epte) had blocks in them and that the lateral trenches off them had been occupied.

3 - 4 pm. (These companies) pushed forward after extremely violent fighting at close quarters, with the result that the enemy suffered very heavy losses and took to flight, effectively pursued by rifle, machine gun and artillery fire.

The rest of the diary concerns itself with the mopping up of the various strong points that the British had established, using all the resources of the 55th and weakened companies from the 170th. Towards midnight elements of the 77th Reserve Regiment were brought into the line. The night was used to restore order in the trenches, get the battalions into their new positions and to erect new wire.

The post mortem that followed the battle was extremely detailed. The Germans felt, for example, that the position was an extremely unfavourable one because of the possibility of enfilade artillery fire on the south sector from Fonquevillers and on the north sector from Hebuterne. The accuracy of the artillery fire on the G5 trenches was particularly noted. Traverses were quite useless, and in future it was recommended that these should be at least ten metres thick to absorb the heaviest of artillery shells. (Traverses in a trench are what distinguishes it from what might be described as a ditch - it provides the distinctive zigzag feature of trenches in aerial photographs and on maps.)

The report noted the impossibility of retaining telephone communication under the heavy artillery fire and the vulnerability of even dugouts which were six metres deep if shelled by heavy calibre howitzers. It goes on,

All the trenches that were bombarded on July 1st were completely flattened out. Only shell holes remained. The wire was unable to withstand the systematic bombardment. Although all damage caused by the bombardment during the day was repaired at night, after the bombardment of July 1st the wire in front of G5, fifty yards wide, had completely disappeared.

The English had excellent maps of our trenches. They were extremely well equipped with bridging ladders, equipment for close fighting, obstacles, machine guns and rations and were well acquainted with the use of our hand grenades.

The report concludes with a comment about the attack, which is a useful balance to the failure that it undoubtedly was.

It must be acknowledged that the equipment and preparation of the English attack were magnificent. The assaulting troops were amply provided with numerous machine guns, Lewis guns, trench mortars and storming ladders. The officers were provided with excellent maps which showed every German trench systematically named and gave every detail of our positions. The sketches had been brought up to date with all our latest work, and the sectors of attack were shown on a very large scale. Special sketches showing the objectives of the different units, and also aeroplane photographs, were found amongst the captured documents.

The report ends on a triumphant note:

July 1st terminated in a complete victory for the 2nd Guard Reserve Division. Every man in the Division is proud of this result and of the success won. The most westerly point of the German line on the Western Front remains intact in our hands. Full of confidence, the brave troops maintain their watch with the same strength and endurance in order to annihilate every fresh attempt on the part of the enemy whenever it may come.

The Division was not to have such a happy time some weeks later at Pozières (see the book of that name in this series).

An explanation of the British failure is rather more complex. In some respects the men were probably over prepared for their task, leading to a lack of initiative, though where initial success was gained this did not seem to be lacking. The poor weather and the consequent physical exhaustion of the troops doubtless played a significant part. The inadequacy of the artillery at this time was possibly the most significant factor, which was resolved as the mobilisation of industry and the experience of the gunners developed. The problem of poor communications meant that commanders were generally ignorant of what was going on and when decisions were made faced a large time gap before orders reached down to the necessary level. What is not an excuse in this particular case was the battle experience of these Territorial divisions. Finally, of course, it was the quality of the German position, carefully selected to withstand assault, supported by first rate second line positions which enabled fire to be brought down over the heads of their comrades in the first, and the high quality of the German troops in the line, that ensured that Gommecourt did not fall to the allied attack.

Chapter Six

A BRIEF CAR TOUR OF THE BATTLEFIELD

This is a simple description of the battlefield area, enabling the visitor to get his or her bearings. It is almost inevitable that the walking part of the tour will also be made much easier if a car is used, especially when it is impossible to cross the fields because of crops.

This tour begins with a cemetery; this is deliberate, because any visit to the battlefield should concern itself with the men who fought and suffered here, most of them believing the cause was just, even if they may well have wished they were miles away. It is an opportunity to pay tribute to those who were killed and also those who survived, often scarred for the rest of their lives. It is all too easy to think about this as an exercise in history and to forget that there are survivors of this conflict still alive (albeit a rapidly dwindling number); whilst elsewhere, in less fortunate parts of the world, conflict remains rife and is as bloody as anything the Great War produced.

Hebuterne Military Cemetery [1] is to the west of the village, up a small country lane, set well off to the right of the road. In the war years this road led to Souastre, but now it degenerates into a track and is not suitable for vehicles. The approach path used to be shaded by trees on one side, but these have recently been cut right back. The cemetery, established in an orchard, was begun by the 48th (South Midland) Division in August 1915 soon after they took over this part of the front from the French. The burials tend to be in divisional and regimental groups and, especially towards the rear, are spaced irregularly. The 56th Division has a large number of burials in the cemetery - for example the London Scottish have large numbers in Plot III, Rows G - H. The carnage of 1 July is reflected in the shared headstones in Plot IV, Row M. The village was occupied for a while by the German in 1918, but the cemetery seems to have got by this further interruption by war relatively unscathed. Captain Richard Seddon is representative of one of the New Zealanders who was killed in this later fighting. He had fought as a young man in the South Africa war; his father was Prime Minister of New Zealand between 1893 and 1906. There are 735 burials in the cemetery, including three Germans (to be found at the rear of the cemetery); there was no concentration of graves after 1918, so this peaceful and tranquil spot is very much a front line cemetery containing the casualties brought here during the war.

From the cemetery head in to Hebuterne; **stop by the shrine [2]**, opposite a large patch of green. This grassed area is the site of the village pond, to which Aubrey Smith makes reference. There is a road to the left of this (a cul de sac) and to the left of that was the area known as the Keep, situated in an orchard, where 7/Middlesex waited to play their part in the Great Push on 1 July. It is worth mentioning that a large number of villages in the Somme area were surrounded by orchards at the time of the Great War; nowadays only the occasional rather apologetic vestige remains.

Before proceeding towards Fonquevillers note the long straight road that is

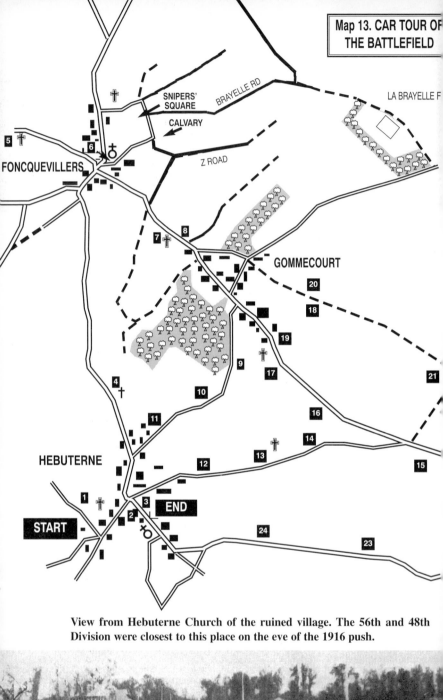

Map 13. CAR TOUR OF THE BATTLEFIELD

BRAYELLE RD

LA BRAYELLE F

SNIPERS' SQUARE

CALVARY

Z ROAD

FONCQUEVILLERS

5

6

7

8

GOMMECOURT

20

18

19

9

17

4

10

16

11

14

HEBUTERNE

13

15

12

1

3

END

START

2

24

23

View from Hebuterne Church of the ruined village. The 56th and 48th Division were closest to this place on the eve of the 1916 push.

In Spring 1918, Germans walk up the snowy village street of Hebuterne, passing on their way a captured British tank.

the main street; this was liable to machine gun fire shooting straight along the street from the German positions before Serre. As the road to Fonquevillers leaves this part of Hebuterne note the **Café des Sports [3]**, at the road junction. Opposite it, in what was then an orchard, was the beginning of Yankee Street.

About a kilometre or so out of Hebuterne, on the right hand side, will be seen a **calvary [4]**. In the rough ground nearby, almost at its furthest, easternmost edge, can be made out a concrete bunker, a British observation post for the German line. The original was constructed in 1916 as part of a series of observation posts along the Somme front; when the fighting returned here in 1918 it was rebuilt by the 42nd (East Lancs) Division. It is wired off, but access is possible with care. From here it there are good views across the front of much of the 56th Division line. The shallow indentation to the left, near the road, is the remnant of what was a track that ran into the Gommecourt road, just outside Fonquevillers, and from a fork in its course also ran along the northern front of Gommecourt Park at the time of the war. The British Z sector was to the north of it, the Y sector to the south.

Proceed in to Fonquevillers; the road was called Thorpe Street. Go up the main street of Fonquevillers and take the left turn, signposted to **Fonquevillers Military Cemetery [5].**

Fonquevillers Military Cemetery.

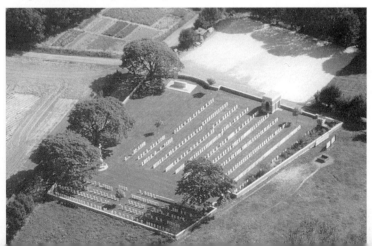

This cemetery was taken over from the French in the summer of 1915, when the British first came here. The 325 French burials were removed after the war and taken to the French National Cemetery at La Targette, not far from the Vimy Memorial Park; for some reason, one remains. This removal of bodies explains the relatively spacious feel to the place, which was sited just beyond the western outskirts of the village, and therefore not in an orchard. Only seventy four graves were brought in after the armistice, although some recent additions have been made. A couple of bodies found after the cemetery was built may be seen by the boundary wall with the road; whilst in the front row is almost the entire crew of a Royal Canadian Air Force bomber from World War II. The sole survivor used to make pilgrimages to the place in post war years. Also of post war vintage are two members of the Chinese Labour Corps, used to clear the battlefields in the immediate post armistice period. They were probably the victims of a munitions explosion.

When the war ended it was far from clear what would happen to the destroyed villages; so devastated was the countryside as well as the villages that at one time it was seriously considered that the area of greatest damage would be left as a memorial to the war. This approach was only changed in the twenties, so that a couple of the regimental histories, published soon after the war ended, could comment on this and approve of the fact that the hallowed ground would be preserved for ever.

A dug-out under the churchyard in Fonquevillers. TAYLOR LIBRARY

Plot I, Row L is particularly full of the casualties of 1 July - with as many as three names on a single headstone. Those officers recovered by the Robin Hoods in March 1917 are buried in Plot III - Captain Walker and Second Lieutenants Flint and Gamble lie side by side in Row E, graves 4 - 6; Captain Leman, obviously found on a different day, is buried in D 10. The only man to win a VC in the 46th Division on the day was Captain John Green of the RAMC attached to 5/Sherwood Foresters. He is buried in Plot III, Row D 15. As for the officers mentioned above, his body was not recovered until the spring of 1917. His citation in the London Gazette for 4 August 1916 reads:

Although himself wounded, he went to the assistance of an officer who had been wounded and was hung up on the enemy's wire entanglements, and succeeded in dragging him to a shell hole, where he dressed his wounds, not withstanding that bombs and rifle grenades were thrown at him the whole time. Captain Green then endeavoured to bring the wounded officer into safe cover, and had nearly succeeded in doing so when he himself was killed.

The man that he attempted to save was Captain Robinson, a machine gun officer. He subsequently died of his wounds and is buried at Warlincourt Halte British Cemetery, along with a number from the 46th Division who were evacuated wounded from the immediate area of the front. Casualties would have been moved from here, using the nearby railway line, if they were capable of undergoing the next stage of the medical evacuation programme.

At the outbreak of the war, recently qualified (although still completing the probationer part of his course), Green was commissioned into the RAMC and was attached for some time to 5/South Staffords, in which regiment his younger brother also served and who was killed in October 1915 at the time of the battalionís attack on Hohenzollern Redoubt. He has no known grave.

Harry Roberts MM, a member of 46th Division Field Ambulance, was one of those who helped to recover Captain Green's body. One of his chief memories of the Somme was being summoned to the Ferme de la Haie, a very large place a couple of kilometres to the west of Fonquevillers. There he found a number of men who appeared to be sleeping but had died as a result of a gas attack during the night.

From the cemetery return to the main street of Fonquevillers and take the road opposite to Gommecourt. Look to the left and on the right hand side of the main street going north will be seen the **village war memorial [6]**. At its base is a simple but poignant memorial to the North Staffs, which has engraved on it their cap badge and the simple statement, Gommecourt July 1st 1916. To commemorate the village's connections with the Sherwood Foresters, the village was adopted by Derby, which city helped with the post war reconstruction. Most years a group of Army Cadets from Nottingham come here and participate with the village in a 1 July commemoration service.

On Easter Sunday, 8 April 1917, Padre Tanner MC* visited the remains of the village.

The village has been very badly knocked about. Not a single house is habitable and most of the men have to be put in dugouts or cellars

Remains of the ancient church at Fonquevillers, taken on 26 May 1917.

under the ruins. The only parts of the church which remain are the four battered walls and a large and absolutely unscathed crucifix. Underneath the Churchyard (now gone) are large subterranean passages, very deep, cold and damp. They were used as bomb stores at one time but are now almost empty. Anyhow, we had to put 150 men into them for want of a better place. Unattractive though it seemed, however, they soon made themselves comfortable with help of braziers. The actual churchyard above is full of big shell holes and coffins and bones are protruding in many places - a truly gruesome place.

He goes on to describe the Easter service in the ruins of the church.

There was certainly no roof and the walls were partly demolished but the floor, though covered with debris, was fairly flat at the east end. The men spent the afternoon sitting out in the open on the grass enjoying the warm sun...At 5 pm the drummer began to play at the cross roads outside the church, and at 5.15 pm the service began. In the absence of packing cases I made the communion table out of fifteen boxes of live bombs covered with a Union Jack. The band stood in a ruined side chapel.

Cross the main street and take the road to Gommecourt and Puisieux. The large British cemetery on the right is **Gommecourt Wood British cemetery [7]**, situated in No Man's Land; opposite it and some twenty or thirty yards in the field, were the ruins of the sucrerie. Looking to the left there is a **metalled track [8]**, which for some time follows the course of the old German front line. Thus the ground between it and the north of the cemetery was the killing ground for the 46th Division on 1 July. Proceed through the village, noting the chateau and church on your right and take a small road on your right which passes alongside the eastern and southern part of Gommecourt Park. Much of the heaviest fighting took place as the road kinks right and then left [9], with trenches such as Fir, Eel, Feast and Fen being more or less adjacent. This is the battleground of the London Rifle Brigade and 2/London Regiment.

See map on page 127

After emerging from the Park (which you leave on the right) the road proceeds through the valley with a gentle bend to the right; the British new line ran about fifty yards after this bend starts. On the right it was marked by **Z Hedge [10],** of which there remains no trace. Continue in to Hebuterne, where the original **British front line [11]** is more or less indicated by the tree line on its outskirts.

Turn left at the road junction and then take the first left, signposted to Gommecourt British Cemetery No 2.

As the road begins to become sunken, there is a turn to the right, going back sharply right; just beyond the junction the old line crossed the road at an angle of 45 degrees; it was to here that stragglers came back from various battalions, the aid post was used as required and others were reorganised before they moved out of the line. On the left hand side of the road and just beyond the old line, the **QWRs [12]** were laid out ready to follow behind the advance of the QVRs and the LRB.

The cemetery [13], some metres further on, is set off the road on your left, more or less on the newly dug British front line; from this area the Rangers launched their attack. During the war there was a track that went off near here to the right, which has now disappeared. Along this track was the junction of W 49 and W48 and it was from here on 31 May 1916 that the panorama pictures found in this book of the German positions were taken.

About a hundred yards before the road bends gently to the right was where the **German line [14]** crossed the road, in this case successively Fate, Fall and Fame, with Et running parallel on the left. Scrubby ground on the right is just below Fame, and British parties penetrated close to this area on a pronounced forward slope by accident on 1 July.

At the crossroads, turn left. The two **British cemeteries [15]** on the right are covered in the rear areas tour. In front of you, before you turn, is Rossignol Wood.

After a kilometre or so, as the road bends gently to the right, there is often on the left a pile of manure or lime stone waiting to be used on the fields. This is the site of **Nameless Farm [16]**, a German strongpoint between their second and third line which caused considerable difficulty to the British advance. After another kilometre the **communal cemetery [17]** will be found on the left. There was very heavy fighting in and around it, especially on its south and south eastern side (Eck). On the opposite side of the road, five hundred yards or so to the north east, was the complex of trenches known as the **Quadrilateral [18]**.

Shortly after leaving the cemetery the road crosses the line of the **Kern (The Maze) Redoubt [19]**, which was a stronghold which roughly included most of

125

the buildings of the village in a heavily fortified position, with many of the cellars of the houses linked up with each other. During the battle there was a garrison of almost 600 Germans in this area. Take the first right turn in the village which will bring you to the north east corner of the redoubt and the south west corner of Gommecourt Wood. At the crossroads, go straight ahead, along a road that is designed for local traffic and access only, and which can on occasion be barred. After five hundred yards or so you will cross the German 1st Switch Line. In the fields to the left ran **Fillet and Fill [20]**, where the two divisions were to join and create a new line. Just beyond, and to the right of the road, was the **Quadrilateral [18]**, and the two communication trenches (first Ems, then Etch) that were used by the QWRs as they made their painful way forward. Etch was some fifty yards further along the road and Epte a hundred yards beyond that. It was down these trenches that the Germans bombed the British out on the orders of **Major Tauscher [21]**, who had come forward to observe the battle from Bucquoy. His observation position was just to the south of the road, near its junction with the Bucquoy road. The large wood off to the left middle distance is **Biez Wood [22],** a site of fierce fighting in 1917. It was much valued by the RFC because of its distinctive arrow shape in the direction of the British line.

At the junction turn right and then take the left turn towards Puisieux, passing Rossignol Wood and Owl Trench cemeteries. In this village, used by the Germans for billeting, turn right and immediately right again, this time on the Hebuterne Road. After about two kilometres, on the right hand side, will be found a large parking area and beyond it a quarry. Quite often, especially in the ploughing and sowing seasons, there are munitions piled up to one side, awaiting disposal. Just beyond the quarry, on a quite sharp leftwards bend, a track led northwards towards Rossignol Wood. The German support line lay parallel to it and about fifty yards to the east.

About a kilometre from the east of Hebuterne there are signs of embankment in the field on the right which marks the line of a now disappeared road towards Puisieux and Rossignol Wood. This road junction area was called **Sixteen Poplars [23]**; about fifty yards beyond this, on the right, was the jumping off position for the London Scottish. They set off north eastwards, as the British line bent back here and ran across the road at right angles. About three hundred yards beyond this was the original British line, and was where the **Kensingtons [24]** waited to make their advance.

Enter Hebuterne (Welcome Street ran parallel to the road here), turn down the main street, past the massive church on the left and stop at the **Café des Sports [3]** for a welcome drink.

Chapter Seven

WALKING TOURS

Walking the 56th (London) Division Battlefield

Parts of the divisional area are covered under the car tour of the battlefield, which should be done first, as some of the descriptions of the route will be found there. This is a simple walk which takes the visitor in a circuit from Hebuterne, past Gommecourt Cemetery No 2, Nameless Farm, Gommecourt communal cemetery, the centre of the village and back to Hebuterne along the road that runs along the southern edge of the Park.

The map used is extracted from the Official History map for the 1 July attack; this will enable the walker to follow events in conjunction with what they will have read in the chapter on the attack by the Division.

I recommend that the car is left in the main street in Hebuterne, near to the Café des Sports. Theft from cars has been quite common, so leaving it beside somewhere near people and with belongings put away in the boot makes such an event less likely.

Map 14. Extract from the Official History Map Attack of 56th Division.

Gommecourt No 2. Note Rossignol Wood on the right. The German Second Line system ran from its west, along the high ground to the left.

Take the road signposted with a green CWGC sign to Gommecourt Cemetery No. 2. The road layout in this sector is broadly similar to that which existed in 1916, so it is possible to see where the various communication and forward trench systems were, even if this requires an effort of imagination! In due course the cemetery is reached.

Gommecourt Cemetery No 2 is one of a number created in this area after the advance to the Hindenburg Line in the spring of 1917. It is situated on the British trench that was dug to bring the two opposing lines closer; Gommecourt No 4 was about a hundred yards to the north west, No 1 about sixty yards to the west of the present cemetery and No 3 was in the south west corner of the village. This latter cemetery was also known as Divisional Cemetery. All of these were concentrated into No 2, along with many other isolated burials, in the post war years. The original burials of No 2 are all in Plot 1 and all of the 56th Division.

Over half of the graves are unknown, and the majority of these are likely to be men from the 56th Division - of the named graves, a very high proportion are from the later fighting of 1916 and 1917.

There are two brothers from the QVRs buried side by side in III B 12. Henry and Philip Bassett were both killed on 1 July, presumably in the ground to the north west of the cemetery, which was the QVR start line. Their parents may have already been dead, as the register only makes reference to their sisters, one of whom married a Frenchman and was living in Paris.

At the rear of the cemetery, in Plot 1V, Row K, there is a line of several men of 2/Honourable Artillery Company, all killed on 15 March 1917 in operations to jolly the Germans along to the Hindenburg Line. Amongst their number [K13] was Joseph Leopold Mann. He was a former pupil of St Edmund's College, Ware, where he arrived as a church student in September 1910 at the age of 14. This meant that he was hoping, in due course, to go on to ordination and the Roman Catholic priesthood. He was recruited under the Derby scheme, the first attempt to deal with the shortage of manpower as the number of volunteers began to dry up. This involved the registration of men eligible for military service. In due course he was called up, and met his end in the spring of 1917.

The main street at Hebuterne. The Café des Sports is on the left of the photograph.

The school magazine reported,

> *The next day his body was found, and from his position we may reconstruct the picture of his passing. He had been shot in the side, and unable to move forward or back, he lay out there under fire, and fell to reading his prayer book. How long he lay there praying we do not know, but a bullet in the head finished his prayer and his work on earth.*

There are good views from the end of the cemetery across the ground covered by the men of the division; and also of Rossignol Wood, where the Germans had their second line.

On the opposite side of the road there used to be a track that ran down to the Puisieux road, but this has now gone. It was from this side of the road that 168 Brigade began its attack, working in a north eastwards direction.

Joseph Leopold Mann and his grave below.

Proceeding along the road the German line is soon crossed. On the right there is some scrubland in an overgrown quarried area which is just behind Fame and Fable, points reached by A and C Company of the London Scottish.

At the cross roads turn left towards Gommecourt. The German third line ran parallel to the road. Stop and look over the British advance from the site of Nameless Farm, imagining the lines of trenches and yards of wire that lay between it and the British - yet the attackers got through to this point. The road continues past the cemetery. It is possible to work your way to the back of the cemetery and see the view enjoyed by the German defenders of the attacking men of the LRB, QVRs and QWRs. Just beyond the cemetery, continuing on the road into Gommecourt, there used to be a small wood, which the Germans called Patrol Wood. Kern Redoubt ran through part of this. All the area up to the church through which you pass was incorporated into this defence work, with its considerable underground shelters. Just before the church is the Mairie, with a simple plaque on the wall commemorating 5/North Staffords. The chateau is beyond the church; it is not a replica of the pre war house, but is still quite a considerable building. The entrance to the old drive through Gommecourt Wood is exactly opposite, though now that has disappeared and is grassed over, though its indentations are clear enough. It was probably used as an exercise for horses and for an afternoon drive for the lady in her horse and carriage.

Continue to the end of the village, looking towards Fonquevillers, but then turn right, which will bring you along the southern end of Gommecourt Wood and the edge of Kern Redoubt. Turn right again, and when you meet the road on which you came into the village, turn left. Shortly afterwards you will come to a narrow road on the right, which you should take. Just before the road makes the first quite sharp right bend look into the fields straight ahead. At this point you are still within the Kern Redoubt, and about 100 yards away was the site of Maze Trench and some of the desperate fighting in the latter hours of the

Above the ruins of the Château de Gommecourt. Left, the rebuilt Chateau as it is today.

British occupation of the German front line positions.

See map on page 56 Continue along the road, having taken the opportunity to look at the map on page 56 which shows the position of the line and of some of the characters mentioned in the section describing the attack of the LRB. Proceed into Hebuterne, past the site of the village pond and back to the Cafè des Sports.

Walking the 46th Division Battlefield

Because of the nature of the tracks, which often stop in the middle of a field, it will probably be necessary to combine the car with the walks around this part of the battlefield.

The start point is Gommecourt Wood Military Cemetery. This cemetery was created after the war by concentrating a large number of small cemeteries in the area; these cemeteries lost their independent existence largely because the numbers buried there were too small and because there was no easily accessible route to them. This procedure did not begin until some time in the early twenties, as a guide to the cemeteries, printed in 1921, has all of them listed and pinpointed on the map with an independent existence.

They are:

Gommecourt church October 1916.

1/5 North Staffordshire Regiment plaque is just above the notice board to the right of the stairs of the Mairie, which is shown left with Gommecourt Church in the background.

A. Gommecourt Chateau Cemetery, begun by the Germans and in which was buried soldiers killed in the 1918 fighting. The German graves were removed elsewhere.

B. Gommecourt Wood No 1 or The Sap Cemetery. This contained 111 men of the 46th Division, nearly all unidentified.

C. Gommecourt Wood No 4 or Little Z containing 22 men of the 46th Division.

D. Gommecourt Wood No 2 - no information in the register

E. Gommecourt Wood No 3 - no information in the register

F. Gommecourt Wood No 5 containing 27 men of the 46th Division

G. Gommecourt Wood No 6 containing the graves of 40 men, mainly from the 46th Division

H. Gommecourt Wood No 8 which contained 46 men from the 46th Division.

I. Point 75, which contained 35 men of the 46th Division

J. Bastion Cemetery which contained 55 men of the 46th Division

K. Poplar British Cemetery - no information in the register

739 men are buried here, of whom 464 are unknown; the vast majority of these would be members of the 46th Division.

As you enter the cemetery there is a plaque on the wall on the right hand side commemorating the 46th Division; after the fiasco of 1 July and the subsequent dismissal of their divisional commander, the division felt that their honour was not fully restored until the storming of the Hindenburg Line in the dying months of the war. Their crossing of the canal at Riqueval was described by Field Marshal Haig as one of the finest deeds of the war, and their main divisional memorial is there.

The Commanding Officer of 5/North Staffords is buried here; Colonel Boote was a pre war Territorial who was the manager of a pottery works. Also buried here is BS Kendrick of 6/South Staffords, in Plot I, Row E, 3. His grave was discovered in 1917 by Padre Tanner. On the evening of his busy Easter Sunday, the RSM of 2/Worcesters (with whom he was serving at the time) came up to him and said that they had found the body of a British soldier in the village and buried him.

I at once decided to walk over to Gommecourt. The RSM went with me and I read the Commital Prayer and Sentence over the newly made

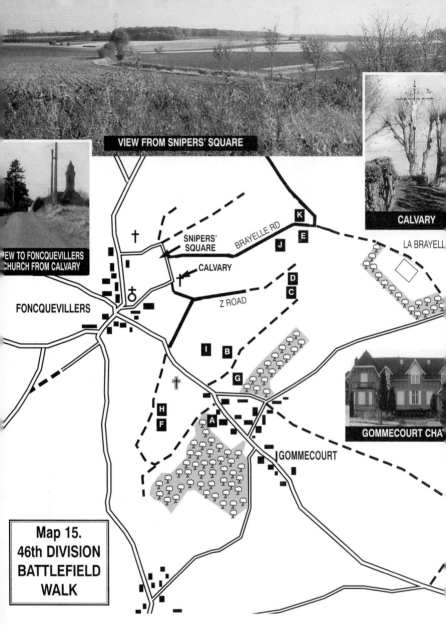

VIEW FROM SNIPERS' SQUARE

CALVARY

VIEW TO FONCQUEVILLERS CHURCH FROM CALVARY

FONCQUEVILLERS

SNIPERS' SQUARE

BRAYELLE RD

CALVARY

Z ROAD

LA BRAYELL

GOMMECOURT CHA

GOMMECOURT

**Map 15.
46th DIVISION
BATTLEFIELD
WALK**

grave. In the stream near by from which the body had been taken I thought I detected another body but as it was getting dark I decided to return next day with the Pioneers.

In fact there is no stream in the region of Gommecourt, so it was probably a flooded part of the valley lying between the two villages. The following day he returned to the spot.

Walked over to Gommecourt this morning with two of the Pioneers

132

and found the second body in the stream. It was a gruesome sight. The skull was in the middle of the water. The trunk was a mass of soft clay and bones. The legs, still in top boots, were also in the stream a few yards away. Closer investigation resulted in the production of the man's knife and pocket book, and also his identity disc tied to a Mill's bomb (grenade). It bore the name of B Kendrick 6th South Staffords. His coat was found also that of a sergeant who was buried last night. The Pioneers put the remains in a grave and I read the Burial Service. I am glad to have obtained identification as it will relieve some anxious relatives who may still be clinging to the hope that the 'Missing' one may still be alive.

Gommecourt Wood Cemetery stands in No Man's Land - more or less opposite was the sucrerie. The line of pylons running off in this field gives a fairly good indication of the British front line, at least for several hundred yards.

Proceed towards Gommecourt and take the metalled track to the left; do not be tempted to drive along this as it gradually degenerates, ultimately into no track at all, and there is nowhere to reverse. This track follows the German front line its entire length, until it disappears. About 300 yards along the track, as it bends to the left, is the site of Gommecourt Wood No 1 or the Sap Cemetery (B), which contained the graves of 111 men of the 46th Division. The War Diary of 6/North Staffords records the following:

March 20 am Salvage. 2pm to Essarts. Before moving the remains of five officers and 68 ORs of the Division who fell in action on 1/7/16 were buried. Position of burial E28 a 90.10.

This was a part of the line where the British managed to make a brief entry, the wire here being comparatively well cut. This rather prosaic entry received more detail in a letter to the Lichfield Mercury.

Cpl Howard T Horobin NSR TF, who has been missing since July 1st at the charge at Gommecourt is now reported killed. Sergeant J Rowley writes, 'He was found in No Man's Land, and has been buried in practically the same spot as he fell. Many other comrades were found too, both officers and men, and they have all been laid to rest together. They were buried on March 20th with full military honours - band, firing party etc. The whole battalion (6/North Staffords) turned out to pay their last tribute to our poor comrades. This is the first funeral I have seen out here where full military honours have been paid. Of course it has not been possible on other occasions.'

'I have never witnessed such an impressive ceremony in all my life, and I do not think I have felt one quite as much as this one. A large cross is being erected over the graves with the names of the fallen inscribed thereon. I am sure every care will be taken to keep these graves in a respectable condition.'

Unfortunately this was something of a pious hope; even Corporal Horobin's

View from German line to the right of The Z – Fonquevillers is on the opposite ridge.

SITE OF POPLAR CEMETERY

L/Cpl 2283 Albert Thomas Weston DCM was a member of Tamworth Territorials who are shown in the photograph above, marching through Burton, August 1914. He was killed in action 1 July 1916.

grave became unidentifiable, and so his name is to be found on the Thiepval Memorial. He was a member of the Tamworth Company of 6/North Staffords; amongst others buried in this cemetery it is possible that Albert Weston DCM found a resting place there as well. Killed on 1 July, he got his DCM for assisting in the rescue of men overcome by gas in tunnels near Wulverghem , under the Messines Ridge.

Just before the point where the track disappears is the part of the line attacked by 5/Sherwood Foresters; it is somewhere about here that Captain Green rescued the wounded officer and was killed in the ground between here and Z Road.

If the ground is solid and there are no crops in the field (the best time for this is the late summer), it is possible to walk across to Z Road. However, it is best to assume that this is not possible, and to retrace your steps to the main road.

Proceed towards Gommecourt and take the track that runs across the northern face of Gommecourt Park. The Park is now a wood - before the war it was much more ornamental, a recreation ground for the chateau owner. Now it is defended by barbed wire and by signs warning of hunting. Although the park is full of relics of the war, it is my advice to keep well out of it unless permission has been secured. The walk starts along the old German line (indeed the troublesome machine gun of 1 July was positioned almost immediately by the road and track junction), and even when, after 400 yards or so, the German line bent back to the south, saps ran out to the track along much of its length.

This track, too, more or less disappears; the concrete bunker on Thorpe Road can be made out about three hundred yards or so away to the south. On the right is a track that leads in towards Fonquevillers. Although it has disappeared for a short distance, it is possible to make out its course, and providing crops are not endangered, it makes an interesting walk back to the Gommecourt Road. Eventually Gommecourt Wood Cemetery comes into view; it does indicate that the ground to the north east of the road was largely out of sight from this side. The British line is crossed more or less where the embankment disappears.

Return to your car at the cemetery.

Attack of the 46th Division continued

Drive towards Fonquevillers; the village marks the limit of the German advance in 1918, and was not captured by them. Take a right turn almost opposite where you emerged from the track before returning to the car. At the next junction turn left, and after a couple of hundred yards stop by the large calvary on the right. Go up to the calvary, which existed during the war. Running almost due east was Rotten Row, and fifty yards north of that was Roberts Avenue. Waiting in assembly trenches across these trenches (and Brayelle Road beyond, again to the north) were the men of 6/Sherwood Foresters. Walk back the way you came in the car, but at the junction carry straight on; this is Z Road. Although it looks promising enough for a vehicle, again the track degenerates until it, too, disappears into a field. After about 400 yards you will cross near the point where 6/North Staffords had their junction with 6/Sherwood Foresters. Approximately where the power lines cross the road was where the jumping off trenches for 5/Sherwood Foresters were, with, on their left, 7/Sherwood Foresters. The Little Z was opposite the point where the track stops, possibly around the edge of the small belt of woodland opposite. If the fields have no crops in them it is possible to make the short crossing to the Brayelle road; otherwise return the way that you came.

See maps on page 80 and 88

Leave the car and continue past the calvary. Take the next turning right, which is the Brayelle Road. Roberts Avenue crossed this almost as soon as you turned right, and Regent Street ran along it for a short distance some three hundred yards further on. Where the power line crosses the road is about one hundred and fifty yards beyond the line of the British attack, but it is roughly the point where the British front was. In the ground of the road junction is the site of Poplar Cemetery. The German position known as The Z came down almost to the point where a track goes off on the left. Climb the bank and one gets a good idea of the German potential for enfilade fire from this strongpoint. A German line ran along the length of this bank, with the front line falling back north eastwards, forming a salient, until it resumed a straight line on the high ground.

Return up the Brayelle Road, and instead of turning left to return to the car, turn right. Note the embankment on the left, and the large quantities of concrete debris. Take the next left and then proceed until a rubbish disposal area becomes apparent. This is often open - go through it and in to the field beyond (gated off). This is the area of Snipers Square, and there is evidence from dowsing of underground workings. The views across the German lines are considerable, and it is probable that it was used both by snipers and observers. On the way back to the car note the railway sleepers forming part of the fencing opposite the entrance to the dump.

Great War railway sleepers and light railway line still having a practical life.

Chapter Eight

THE REAR AREAS

This tour takes the visitor through the villages to the west and north west of the battlefield that were used by the British as billets. There is little indication of the war in them, apart from the guns (for example at Berles au Bois) or shells that surround war memorials, and a number of British cemeteries. However some of them are still small villages, with wattle and daub walled barns in the French style - ie the barns forming the frontage to the street and the gates open to reveal the farm house at the back. Gone, thank heavens, is the great midden that seems to have been a chief characteristic in the war days. Driving along some of these roads is to see parts of the Somme as the soldiers saw it - the roads might not be so sunken or so rough, power lines might disfigure the landscape and the fields are larger, but for all that there is a bygone feel about

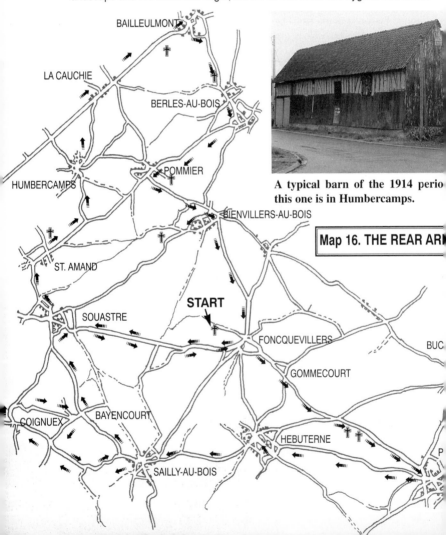

A typical barn of the 1914 period this one is in Humbercamps.

Map 16. THE REAR AR

this relatively unpopulated part of France, charming in the summer, tremendously bleak on a dank, misty autumnal or winter day.

The tour includes as many as possible of the villages mentioned in the text - most used by several of the units named - but some, such as Lucheuex, are too far to be included here. However, a diversion would not take a motorist too long, especially if an afternoon has been set apart for this part of the battlefield tour.

The tour starts in **Fonquevillers** at the Military Cemetery there. In the main street turn right and follow the D6 to **Souastre**. This road was relatively freely used, at least until the attack on 1 July. Just beyond the D3 turning to Sailly au Bois, about two hundred yards, was the right hand end of Midland Trench, a support line where men of 5/Lincolns and 8/Middlesex waited to be deployed. The trench stretched northwards almost to the Bienvillers road. A track going off to the left leads down to the Ferme de la Haie; this point was known as the Souastre Fork and provided an alternative (night time) route to Bayencourt.

The road reaches a high point before entering Souastre. Somewhere in the field off to the left my grandfather, then serving with the 7th (Service) Battalion Leicestershire Regiment in the 37th Division, sat watching the battle for Gommecourt and his fellow members of the Leicesters, the 4th and 5th battalions. 7/Leicesters was part of 110 Brigade, which formed the Leicestershire Brigade of Kitchener volunteers.

In Souastre head north for **St Amand**, an important billeting area. Soon after entering the village turn right for Pommier, but at the eastern end of St Amand take a small diversion to the left, following the sign to St Amand British Cemetery. This is a small cemetery used by Field Ambulances, by units who managed to bring out their dead from the front line area, and was heavily used in 1918 at the time of the German advance and in subsequent months. Those killed in 1916 are all to be found in Plot I; a high proportion of these were members of 3 (City of London Battalion)/London Regiment. There are 222 UK burials (three unidentified), one from New Zealand and one from India, a member of an ammunition column whose home was Mungwa, Fyzabad, United Provinces. One can only wonder what these men from India made of a war which is known to some Indian historians not as the First World War but as the Great European Civil War.

Return to the Pommier road and after a kilometre or so take the D26 to Humbercamps, another village used by units of the 46th Division for billeting. Follow the road through **Humbercamps**, taking the turning to **La Cauchie**, where you should turn right towards **Bailleulmont**. As you drive along this road look to your left; over this ground, to the west of Arras, some of the heavy fighting

Ruined church at Bienvillers au Bois. 30 June 1917.

Panorama of Hebuterne from the Sailly au Bois road.

took place in May 1940 in the epic struggle to hold the Germans up undertaken by Frankforce. Ferme de la Bezeque, to the south west, was used by Luftwaffe pilots as an officers mess for a nearby fighter airfield.

As you approach Bailleulmont notice on the left, amidst the trees, the ruins of a Donjon; this is an early medieval castle or keep, used to impress and overawe the locals. English dungeon is derived from this French word, and is indicative of the practical use to which most of them were put. Just before entering the village there is a narrow road that bends back sharply to the right. This is a cul de sac that leads to the local communal cemetery in which there is a CWGC plot.

Bailleulmont was also used as a billet by units of the 46th Division, but none of their dead are buried in this small plot which has the unusal brown-red gravestones used in more isolated cemeteries by the CWGC as an experiment to aid maintenance in the early eighties. It contains the well known grave of Private A Ingham who was executed by the army on 1 December 1916. His father insisted, after prolonged correspondence with the authorities, that the stone should be inscribed, *Shot at Dawn*. It goes on, 'One of the first to enlist. A worthy son of his father'. Full details of this, and other capital courts martial resulting in executions, may be read in J Sykes and J Putkowski's, *Shot at Dawn*. Without entering into the heated controversy on this matter, it is interesting to note that the British executed some 350 men during the war (the figure is open to some debate); recent revelations from the Soviet archives show that her army shot over 14,000, that is the size, more or less, of a British division, apparently quite legally, during the Siege of Stalingrad alone.

Bailleulmont is one of the villages with some housing that would have been quite familiar to the soldiers of the Great War, being more or less undamaged by the conflict. This is true of the next three villages which are on the route.

On leaving the cemetery return to the main road and proceed into the village and take the first turning on the right. Follow this road around and take the first turning on the right which will take you to **Berles au Bois**. At a junction there is a British cemetery in which is buried Brigadier General FW Lumsden VC CB DSO (the VC takes priority over all other decorations, civil and military), of the Royal Marine Artillery.

Proceed through the village. Berles, and its near neighbour Bienvillers, were

CQMS AC Cave's billet site, on the right of the photograph, in Bienvillers.

the front line villages for members of 110 (Leicesters) Brigade for many months between August 1915 and June 1916. My grandfather recorded in his diary playing in an inter-battalion rugby match which had to be stopped when a shell landed in the field of play in the second half. The band used to play on occasion in the main street towards the southern end where there is a fork in the main street.

At the southern end of the village take the D30 to **Pommier**, fairly secure from German shell fire. In the communal cemetery (a left turn as you enter the village) is a communal cemetery. German shell fire killed and mortally wounded a number of members of 123rd Brigade Royal Field Artillery on 3 February 1916, and they are buried here. My grandfather (who was not a notable drinker) records spending a night here in his time on this front and waking up the following day, with a number of his friends, to find the floor covered with empty champagne bottles. In the middle of Pommier turn left (the D8) for **Bienvillers**. Turn right at the church there, noting the somewhat dilapidated French 75s flanking the war memorial. This road (the D2) will takes you to the large Bienvillers Military Cemetery. This was started by 110 Brigade when they were in the sector, and the graves are buried more or less chronologically, in divisional and sometimes regimental groups. Amongst those buried here is Lieutenant Colonel Walter Brodie VC MC, killed on 23 August 1918 who won his VC as a lieutenant in the First Battle of Ypres on 11 November 1914.

Turn around and return to Bienvillers and from there take the road to Fonquevillers, which was used so often by the men of the 46th Division. Drive through the village to Gommecourt and proceed through to **Puisieux** on the D6. This part is explained in more detail in the earlier touring section, but much of the road runs parallel to the old German front line and men of the 56th Division reached most of that line on and around the road. Just beyond the crossroads, on the right hand side, are two cemeteries separated by a few hundred yards.

The photograph shows all that was left in Puisieux after the retreating Germans in March 1917. TAYLOR LIBRARY

The first is Rossignol Wood, which was originally established by the 46th Division burial officer in the actions in March 1917 following the German retreat. Most of the men are from 1/5th North Staffs or 1/5th South Staffs. It is highly unusual in that there are more Germans buried here than British, 70 of them. The cemetery is in a hollow, and suffered badly from flooding, so that recently the whole has been almost completely rebuilt. The wood opposite was an important position in 1916, but more famously in 1918, where it is the central landmark in Ernst Junger's, *Copse 125*, a most important piece of Great War literature by a German. Junger was not only a great survivor in the war, at the time of writing (1998) he is still alive. In 1918 the New Zealand Division was in the vicinity - they had stopped the German advance in this area during the spring offensive of 1918.

To the left was where the Germans brought up some field guns to catch men of 56th Division in enfilade. Owl Trench, the second cemetery, was a German trench. There are 53 men buried here, of whom ten are unknown. 43 are from 16/West Yorks, killed attacking the withdrawing Germans in February 1917. Thus this is almost 'their' battlefield cemetery. Note a number of the graves are doubles - ie more than one man is buried under a headstone, equally indicative of the circumstances of their burial.

In Puisieux turn right on to the main road and a few yards later turn right again on the D27 to **Hebuterne**. This road, at the Hebuterne end, formed the extreme right of the 56th Division attack on 1 July 1916, the London Scottish holding this position. Go in to Hebuterne, following the main road. Towards the end of the main street take a left turn, following the sign for Hebuterne Military Cemetery; however do not, in due course, turn up to this, but remain on the road for **Sailly au Bois**. To the left is where the infantry used to make their way in to the village, keeping off the road. Just before coming in to Sailly au Bois is the area where the wagons of men like Aubrey Smith were delayed to avoid German artillery fire. In Sailly keep on the D27 to **Coigneux** (notice the British cemetery on your left); as you drive along this road there is a steep rise to your right which provided the protected route to the front, and was known as Happy Valley (one of many on the Somme). Wooded areas and quarries would have supplied shelter for various units as well as artillery. Coigneux was the village where Smith says that many units brought their horses for watering due to its absence elsewhere. In Coigneux turn right (towards **Souastre**) and soon afterwards right again, towards **Bayencourt**, Aubrey Smith's billeting area and where he had some close encounters with guns. It does not look as though it may have changed all that much in eighty years or so. In Bayencourt turn right, heading back towards Happy Valley - Smith commented on the difficulty of preventing the wagons from running into each other down the steep slope. At the road junction turn left, returning along Happy Valley towards Sailly; before reaching this village take the D129 to **Bayencourt** - the route that Smith decided to use one night to save time (and a hard climb up a hill) but was not, on reflection, such a bright idea. At the crossroads continue on to **Souastre** and from there back to **Fonquevillers**.

FURTHER READING

There is an enormous amount of literature on the Somme. What is offered below can merely be taken a as sample of what is either still in print or readily available from the second hand market.

The First Day on the Somme, Martin Middlebrook. This is one of the great books about the first day of any battle, and one of the first to make use of personal accounts; probably still the most successful of its type. *The Somme,* A H Farrar-Hockley. An excellent overview of the whole battle by both a distinguished general and academic, who is also responsible for the Official History of the Korean War and a biography of Gough. *Somme,* Lyn Macdonald. A highly readable account of the battle, making extensive use of personal recollections. *The 1916 Battle of the Somme: A reappraisal*, Peter Liddle. This book takes into account some of the revisionist writing by academics, who have now begun to move from the blanket 'butchers and bunglers' condemnation of British commanders.

There is a whole range of guides to the Somme battlefields.

By far the best general guide to the memorials, cemeteries and what remains along the old British front line (though it does extend down to and include Verdun) is the late Rose Coombs, *Before Endeavours Fade,* which has been reprinted and revised extensively over the years that it has been in publication. An essential vade mecum for the tourer. Martin and Mary Middlebrook have produced a superb and readable guide to the area, *The Somme Battlefields.*

Major and Mrs Holt's Battlefield Guide to the Somme is relatively new. It is profusely illustrated, follows suggested routes with timings, and comes complete with a most helpful map indicating all the places of interest, cemeteries, memorials and so forth. It is an encyclopaedic survey of what remains on the battlefield.

Paul Reed's *Walking the Somme* is published in this series, and offers a range of walks all over the Somme battlefield, including one at Gommecourt. It is well illustrated, full of information and provides good, clear sketch maps to follow.

Autobiographical accounts have been specifically mentioned, as appropriate, in the body of the book.

Selective Index